Night Light © 2021 by David Campbell

All rights reserved. No part of this publication may be reproduced, distributed, or transmitted in any form or by any means, including photocopying, recording, or other electronic or mechanical methods, without the prior written permission of the publisher or author, except in the case of brief quotations embodied in critical reviews and certain other noncommercial uses permitted by copyright law. For permission requests, email the publisher or author at addresses below:

Contact the author:
www.davidhcampbell.com

Contact the publisher:
DC Christian Publishing
trinitycc@rogers.com

Scripture quotations are from the ESV® Bible (The Holy Bible, English Standard Version®), copyright © 2001 by Crossway, a publishing ministry of Good News Publishers. Used by permission. All rights reserved.

ISBN-978-1-7773978-2-1

Printed in the United States of America
Ingram Printing & Distribution, 2021

First Edition

NIGHT LIGHT

HOW TO FIND GOD
IN THE MIDST
OF SUFFERING

DAVID CAMPBELL

"Light dawns in the darkness for the upright"

(Psalm 112:4)

TABLE OF CONTENTS

Author's Preface   i
Introduction   iii

Chapter 1: The unexpected path to true worship — *Sarah Taylor*   5
Chapter 2: Rooms in the House of Grief — *Franklin Pyles*   19
Chapter 3: Putting the foundations in place   29
Chapter 4: Pathway to hope   41
Chapter 5: The woman who found the well — *Sue Buzzeo*   51
Chapter 6: Suffering and the sovereignty of God   59
Chapter 7: The way of the cross   69
Chapter 8: God didn't promise me a son — *Malyn Sneed*   75
Chapter 9: When Jesus doesn't show up   87
Chapter 10: Overcoming disillusionment   95
Chapter 11: Finding Jesus in the valley of tears — *Philip Logan*   103
Chapter 12: Life in the Refiner's Fire   115
Chapter 13: Keeping faith through the fire   123
Chapter 14: The gateway between earth and heaven — *Sarah Galloway*   139
Chapter 15: Suffering as the birthplace of joy   149
Chapter 16: Is my suffering caused by my sin?   159
Chapter 17: Finding peace in the fire — *Kim Jones*   169
Chapter 18: The power of giving thanks   181
Chapter 19: Count it all joy   189
Chapter 20: So many battles, such great faithfulness — *Pat Westcott*   197
Chapter 21: Learning to remember   207
Chapter 22: Suffering and failure   213
Chapter 23: Suffering for doing right: the reality of spiritual warfare   221

The Last Word   229
About the Author   233
Other Titles   234

AUTHOR'S PREFACE

I have a number of people to thank, primarily those who have had the courage, at considerable emotional cost, to record their stories in these pages, sometimes in the knowledge they might not live to see the book published. Sadly, for two of them that has proven to be the case. As always, I am indebted to my wife Elaine for the many hours she has sat alone while I have worked on the manuscript, and for the wisdom she has offered me, often birthed out of sacrifice and suffering, from the well of her own deep fellowship with Christ. I want to thank the congregation of Trinity Christian Church, Owen Sound, Ontario, which over the years listened to a lot of messages on this theme without ever complaining. I am grateful to Josh Best and his extraordinary creative team at davidandbrook.com for producing this book to such a high standard. This is now our fourth collaboration and hopefully not the last. And lastly, thanks to my friend Evan Sustar of Anderson, South Carolina, for careful proofreading of this book.

And of course, as always, soli Deo gloria — glory to God alone.

INTRODUCTION

Churches have a mixed record in responding to the issue of suffering. We do a reasonably good job of caring for people who are experiencing suffering. It's a big advantage to have a church community around you when things go wrong in your life, and I've witnessed that countless times. But when it comes to teaching on suffering from a Biblical perspective, we generally fall short. I think many preachers are so scared of getting it wrong they handle the subject superficially or hardly at all. And then we wonder why people go off the rails when someone comes along and does tackle the subject, but from a wrong perspective. Avoiding the subject doesn't cause it to disappear!

Part of understanding suffering, as any pastor knows, is the willingness to listen to the stories of those who have suffered. But we also need a firm handle on Biblical truth. Suffering is common to the human condition, and it is to that condition the Bible so powerfully speaks. The plan I felt God gave me for this book was to take stories of people I knew who had gone through suffering and found God in it, and to intersperse them with teaching on how Scripture addresses those experiences, thus bringing God's light into our darkness.

The book was long finished and lying dormant on my laptop when our daughter Sarah's story began, and the rubber hit the road for our own family. That's where this book starts. I hope by the time you have finished it, your ability to grapple with the issues raised in it will have increased, and your faith will rise as you see how God in his grace has met the people whose stories are about to unfold.

CHAPTER 1

THE UNEXPECTED PATH TO TRUE WORSHIP

Sarah Taylor

My phone rang in the middle of a video chat with Jacob. I had programmed my ENT specialist into my contacts, so I knew exactly who it was when I picked up. My heart was racing. Please, good news. It was not good news.

"Unfortunately, it is thyroid cancer."

"Okay. Okay. Okay." were the only words coming out of my mouth but tears were already starting to flow down my face. I kept shaking my head so Jacob could see something was wrong.

Not good, I typed.
Malignant? He typed.
Yes, I typed back.

I could see our dreams being dashed on the rocks, our plans being swept out to sea. I'm stuck here. I have cancer? But I'm only 25? When will I see Jacob? Oh God, am I going to die? It's too soon, I'm too young. These thoughts churned with the tides of tears that coursed down my face. There is nothing in my life that has compared with the sickening, breath-pulled-out-of-your-lungs feeling of being told I have cancer. The questions that arise are like great drowning waves of panic and despair. I couldn't sleep that first night. How could this be part of God's plan?

Jacob and I met in 2019. His parents were old family friends who lived in England. We connected on Instagram after we had both recently left long-term relationships. The chemistry was instant, and within twenty-four hours we were sharing our entire life testimonies with each other. That summer felt like a hazy dream of shifting from work to school to six or seven-hour long video calls with Jacob, who was working at the time for a family in Germany to improve his language skills. I had moved back in with my parents at the beginning of 2019 to pursue my graduate level diploma in art therapy.

The 2019-2020 school year was Jacob's year abroad, living in Vienna, Austria and working as a teaching assistant as part of his university degree. He had a brief ten-day window in September 2019 where he would fly home to England from his work in Germany before flying back out to Austria to begin his year abroad. I flew from Canada to England to meet him, and by the end of that blissful time together we were certain that we were meant to be married. We began planning for our wedding on June 27, 2020 — one year to the day since we had started speaking with each other.

Of course, he had yet to officially propose and we couldn't wait too long before being together again, so we planned for him to spend ten days in Canada in February 2020, a four month wait away. My days were spent starting to plan our wedding, working, and preparing to move to England. It felt like years had passed before I found myself waiting in arrivals at Toronto Pearson Airport. At last, I spotted Jacob's tired face in the crowd, ran to him, and we embraced. He dropped down on one knee right there in the airport and asked me to marry him. Of course I said yes!

Our ten days were up all too soon and, tears streaming down my face, I left Jacob walking through security to catch his flight. I barely noticed the TV monitors in the background talking about this new virus in China, and consoled myself by counting down the days until I would see him again in another four months, at the beginning of June.

As the year progressed, the world began to burn with news of COVID-19. All at once, things changed. Austria locked down and Jacob caught one of the last flights back to England. The virus spread like wildfire. In the middle of March 2020, Canada closed the borders to all "non-essential" travel. Just for a month. There is no way that this will last until June, I thought.

How wrong I turned out to be.

Early in May, Jacob's flight to Canada was cancelled. The borders remained shut. We decided that we would have to postpone our wedding indefinitely unless I flew to England. Britain's borders were not shut, and I began to plan to leave and get married in England. It might be a few weeks delayed, I thought, but at least we will be together.

Then one night in May, as I was washing my face before bed, I felt a small lump on the side of my neck. Something dropped in the pit of my stomach, and I immediately asked my mum to look at it. It could be nothing, we determined, but if it's still there in a week we will get it checked out. My family doctor took my blood, sent me for an ultrasound and a CT scan, and told me it was likely nothing. My bloodwork was fine, my thyroid looked fine, and I had no symptoms. In fact, I was drinking kale smoothies every morning and running seven kms every other day. I was in the best shape of my life. But just to be safe, he sent me to a local ENT specialist, who scheduled a biopsy to get a definitive answer as to why I had a swollen lymph node. I felt certain that as soon as the biopsy came back negative, I would be able to fly to England and be with Jacob.

I wrote a letter to my local Member of Parliament explaining my situation — I should have been married to Jacob, but he is not allowed into Canada, and is there anything that can be done about this? The response was kind, but he noted that no exemptions were in place to the border rules. I began to take to Twitter to express the view that unmarried couples deserved to be reunited in the same way married couples were. If you didn't have a marriage certificate, you would be denied entry. I found that there were hundreds, and then thousands of people in my situation.

On June 25, two days before what should have been my wedding day, I went in for an excisional biopsy. They had me under local anesthetic, meaning I was awake the whole time. What should have been a forty-five minute procedure turned into nearly two hours. At one point, a blood vessel burst and I felt like I was choking. It was incredibly traumatic. The surgeon, a new graduate, had not done a lot of complex biopsies and sent me home with nothing but Tylenol for the pain. The collar of my dress was coated in a necklace of bright red blood. I wandered through the hospital halls to find the exit. I was so light headed that even though my parents were waiting for me, I had to sit in the car for several minutes before driving home. The pain was so intense I could barely speak, and my dad had to call my family doctor and get an emergency order of prescription pain medication. This was not going according to plan. But it's over, I thought. The worst is done. The doctor told me I would have the results in two to three weeks. Seven days later, on July 2, my phone rang.

I thank God that Jacob was on a video call with me at that moment, as it saved me from having to explain it all to him later. While he looked up information to call the Canadian High Commission in London, I stumbled down the stairs and fell into my dad's arms, hyperventilating and crying so hard I was almost screaming. I couldn't even get the words out. My parents held me up as I told them it was cancer. It made no sense to me. I had no family history of thyroid problems, let alone cancer. I had no symptoms, I was perfectly healthy, I was only 25, and this was the worst possible timing. I should have been newly married and on my honeymoon, not collapsed on the couch thinking I might die. My little (but six-foot tall) brother hugged me, my tears soaking his t-shirt, as he told me that nothing was allowed to hurt me because I was his big sister. In the coming days, although God did not spare me from pain, he surrounded me and collected my tears as I walked through the most difficult season of my life.

I received an email address for a reporter from a friend in an online advocacy group. I sent an email, not really expecting to hear back. Jacob's calls, my emails, everything had been fruitless. All we were told is that rules are rules, and they would not make an exception for Jacob to enter Canada. I reached out to my local MP again in desperation. Then my phone vibrated; the reporter wanted to call me. Just days after my diagnosis, I spent nearly an hour on the phone describing our circumstance, how the government wasn't making an exception for Jacob, and the pain we were going through. I didn't know if it would make it to print, but I prayed that God would bring good out of it. Days later, my phone buzzed again. A friend had sent me a message, "Did you know you are currently on the front page of a national newspaper, and trending on Twitter?" My heart raced. Sure enough, we had made headlines. I started getting messages from reporters on local, national and international news stations. I had thirty followers on Twitter in May, but by the end of July, I had hit a thousand. Our story blew up. We appeared on TV programs, live national news, making front pages of local and national newspapers. There was no question about it, God was doing something. In one radio show, the host declared, "She's tapped into something." He was right. As I poured out my heart to God, not understanding why I was in this terrible situation, I felt the need to keep declaring his goodness. In the midst of cancer, five months and counting separated from my fiancé, and an indefinitely postponed wedding, God was faithful. He was still working.

The surgeon who performed my biopsy scheduled my surgery for August 5. I was sent for more scans and tests, and then in the middle of July I received another heart-wrenching phone call. Once again, I was on a video call with Jacob when it happened. The cancer had spread into the left side of my neck, making surgery much more complicated, and requiring a thoracic surgeon to be on standby, which my local hospital could not provide, and my young surgeon felt it was beyond her competence to perform. The surgery was cancelled, and I was referred to a more experienced surgeon in a teaching hospital an hour's drive away in London, Ontario. This truly felt like a step back. If the cancer had spread within weeks, I wanted to have surgery as soon as possible. There is no worse feeling than knowing cancer is growing by the day inside of you, and not knowing when it will be removed.

Traveling has always been challenging for me, and I have suffered from severe travel anxiety since I was a teenager. Anything over thirty minutes meant I need to be medicated. The one-hour drive would have been nothing to most people, but it was extremely challenging for me. Nevertheless, God met me. I did not have a single full-fledged panic attack on any journey I made to that hospital over the months I had to go back and forth. I met with my new surgeon shortly thereafter, and I told her that I was incredibly anxious to have the surgery done. Her schedule was restricted due to the pandemic and she was booking into September and October, but I told her that if a last-minute opening came up, I would be there. I left feeling discouraged. I went for a walk that evening, and felt God reveal something very clearly to me: *my emotions do not dictate his character.* No matter how I feel, God is unchanging. He is always good and always faithful.

On July 31, I got a call from my surgeon: could I come for the surgery on Wednesday at 6 am? — only five days away! I replied with an enthusiastic yes. My new surgery date was August 5, exactly the same day my original surgery had been planned. God works even in the small things.

Jacob and I continued to press into the media, taking every opportunity we could. Suddenly, I had MPs private messaging me on Twitter. My local MP stood up in Parliament and questioned the government about my case. He referred to me by name. Not many people can say that their name has been mentioned in Parliament, but God used the situation we were in to shine a light politically on thousands of separated cross-border families. I quickly became a spokesperson. The Minister of Public Safety knew my name. The Minister of Health knew my name. The Minister of Immigration knew my name. The Prime Minister knew my name. Other Members of Parliament from several parties took up my cause. I began a handwritten letter campaign, writing every single day by hand to politicians, ministers and the Prime Minister — anyone who could effect change in this policy and allow for compassion within the border restrictions. I started the first day with four letters. By the end of my campaign, I had written 132.

The morning of August 5 came quickly. I woke up at 4:30 am to make it to the hospital for 6. Due to COVID-19 restrictions, I had to enter the hospital alone, and was not allowed any visitors. Dad dropped me off just before 6 am, with the sun just beginning to rise. There was a long hallway before the entrance. Before I went in, I turned back and waved to my dad. He waved back. Both of us were pretty broken. "God please help me, I'm alone," I thought. The "what if's" consumed me. What if I don't wake up, what if something goes wrong, what if February 8 was the last time I would ever see Jacob? I stood for a moment in the hallway, tears forming in my tired eyes, and that small whisper came to me, "I am with you." I knew it was the Lord. What I was discovering is that my feelings and my emotions do not dictate my faith. Faith is taking that step through suffering, even if you are hurting beyond what any words can describe. And God gave me faith to keep going that day.

I was so anxious my hands were shaking. Tears were flowing down my face and dripping off my chin like a leaky faucet. For a few minutes, I was left just outside the operating room, waiting for the surgeon to finish preparing. I have never felt fear as real as I did in those moments. All I could do was cry out to Jesus. That was all I had in those moments — only Jesus. I never realized how narrow and hard an operating table is, or how big the lights are, or how hard it is to actually breathe into the mask they put over your face. God help me. God help me. I laid on my back and everything was spinning, spinning, spinning, for what felt like an eternity. How long is it going to be until I pass out? Then I woke up.

I don't like recalling my two days in hospital. They were filled with hours of lying immobile, too weak to make it to the bathroom, having to call a nurse to help me out of bed and onto a portable toilet. My blood pressure dropped, my calcium dipped, my nausea increased. It was a roller coaster of symptoms. I couldn't sleep because the person next to me had a feeding tube that loudly suctioned every two hours. I had two drains in my neck. The tubes sticking out either side made it impossible to turn my head at all. And then I got to go home. They told me the surgery was successful but that I would still need a form of radiation, a one-dose treatment called radioactive iodine. That would come much later on.

My incredible sixty-year-old mum looked after me, doing everything from sponge-bathing me to helping me to the bathroom. Good thing she had been trained a registered nurse! As a twenty-five year old woman, this was one of the most humbling experiences I have faced. And the emotional pain was just as great as the physical pain. Jacob should have been my care-giver. He should by that point have been my husband. Sometimes I was in such pain I had tears rolling down my face, unable to sob because of the pain of the seven-inch incision on my neck. I just wanted to hold Jacob's hand. I just wanted his presence. I just wanted him beside me. I felt so helpless. But the God who was with me in those moments in the hospital hallway was with me there too. In the depth of my pain, I could do nothing but trust that God had a plan and a purpose in all this. I came down with an intense ear infection five days after surgery. I lay in bed, weeping and in pain. I didn't have Jacob, but I did have the presence of the Holy Spirit. I wish I could say that I never felt anything except at peace, but God had other plans. He had me live with my pain, and I couldn't understand why. Yet it brought me to my knees every day, in desperation learning the hard truths of suffering, and crying out to God again and again to make it stop.

I continued to press on, handwriting letters to politicians, advocating on social and news media. Jacob and I had been separated for seven months when in September I got word that exemptions were coming. Hints were given, but the process and the progress were tightly guarded. We didn't know when or how. In this place of complete unknown, all we could do was trust the Lord was working.

My pathology report came back in late August. They had removed my entire thyroid and completed a left, right, and central neck dissection. Fifty-six suspicious lymph nodes were analyzed, but only six came back cancerous. The tumour on my thyroid was only nine mm in diameter. I had the normal variant of the most curable strain, meaning that once the cancer was gone, there'd be a 99% chance it would never come back. And all the spread into the left side of my neck? There was no cancer there. They removed dozens of lymph nodes, and not a single one was cancerous. I wonder whether God made those lymph nodes swell up and appear cancerous so that I would be referred to a better surgeon, one of the best in the country! God is merciful. He allowed me to have cancer, but I had the most curable type, the most normal variant, and my pathology report was amazing. It was the first time I'd received good medical news, and it felt great. The cancer wasn't gone yet, but I was on my way. I came to the realization that I had a world-class team of surgeons operate on me, that I was incredibly lucky to have been referred to this hospital. Of course, luck had nothing to do with it. It was God. Even when the cancer had spread and my surgery was cancelled, he was just using that circumstance to bring me to the best surgeon and the best care I could have received.

On October 2, I awoke to another day of unknowns. It was Jacob's birthday, a day we had dreamed about spending together married. It soon became apparent that today was not like every other day. News releases began to hint about a border announcement that day. A nationally-televised press conference was scheduled in the afternoon featuring the Ministers of Public Safety, Health, and Immigration. A local reporter stopped by at the house to capture the moment. It couldn't be true… yet could it? My stomach was in knots waiting for the press conference to begin when my phone rang. A blocked number. I picked it up, wondering who this might be.

"Hello?"
"Hi, is this Sarah?"
"Yes."
"This is the Minister of Immigration. I am about to make an announcement that will make you very happy."

My jaw dropped and I stumbled over my words. I tried thanking him and blubbered out that it was Jacob's birthday today and this was the best possible gift. Our conversation ended, and I turned to the livestream. I could almost hear the angels in heaven rejoicing as the Minister whom I had just spoken to appeared on national television and announced that all extended family members, including partners and fiancés, would be allowed into Canada. For the first time in a very, very long time,

I was weeping tears of joy. And then something amazing. As he was wrapping up the announcement, the Minister said this, "And to Sarah Campbell, I know you've waited a long time for this, and I am happy to be making this announcement today, on Jacob's birthday." The local reporter who was capturing all of this happening snapped a picture of me, overcome with tears of joy, one hand over my sobbing mouth and the other on my heart. And of course, Jacob was on a video call with me as all of this was happening. God's timing is perfect. From the deepest pain came the greatest joy. We booked his flight.

The application was released on October 7. We were told the approval would be instantaneous, and so we booked the wedding venue for October 25. Jacob would have to arrive by October 10 to finish quarantine in time for the wedding. But by October 9, nothing had happened. Surely God had not brought us this far just to let us down now! I was in contact with the head policy maker at Immigration Canada, who told me the whole department was working to get Jacob's application approved. We set a timer: 5 pm our time, 10 pm Jacob's time, and if we hadn't heard anything we would have to cancel his flight the next day, and cancel our wedding again. At 5 pm, I received an email from my local MP saying he and his staff were fighting hard for us, and to wait until 6 pm to call it. So we gave it one more hour. At 5:40 pm, twenty minutes before we were going to cancel Jacob's flight, the approval came through. Jacob packed his bag and got ready to leave for the airport early the next morning. I cried and hugged my mum. I couldn't believe it was actually happening.

To be honest, I felt like it wouldn't be real until Jacob made it through immigration at the airport. In the end, he was the very first person to enter Canada under the new exemption process. The border guard took one look at Jacob, recognized him from all of the news reports we had been in, and waved him through, saying all the guards knew who he was. Dad picked him up and brought him home. We first saw each other outside, by the mailbox where I had mailed all 132 letters. It had been 245 days since I last saw him, just over eight months, and 100 days since I was diagnosed with cancer. We had been mentioned six times in Parliament, and in local, national, and international media so many times I lost count. And it all came down to this moment. Dad pulled up and Jacob got out of the car. I nearly knocked him over with the force of my embrace! Masks on, we held each other. What God has brought together, let no man separate. All of the borders, the rules, the cancer, and the distance could not separate us forever. God had a plan. On October 25, we were married.

I made it through the remainder of my treatment, including several days where I was considered radioactive! When I returned to the hospital for a full body scan, which records how much cancer is left, I got more good news. The doctor took me into the back room, sat down, and just said, "This is remarkable." He couldn't see any cancer left in my neck. With the caveat that my antibody levels and nine-month followup scan needed to be clear, I was released to move to England and at last begin my new life with Jacob. So I packed my life into three suitcases, flew across the ocean, and that's where I am today. I do not yet know if I am "cancer free," but I have complete faith and trust in God that he will bring me through whatever comes next.

At the beginning of the lockdowns and the pandemic, I began to go on walks with my mum. Once a day, every day. At first we did it to just get out of the house and the news and the drudgery of everything being closed. But it became a ritual that every day we would go on a walk. It didn't matter if there was rain, snow, hail, mud, or sunshine. It didn't matter if we walked around the block or on an eight km trail. We kept walking through my cancer diagnosis, through the long days of uncertainty, scans, tests, and two surgeries (with a few days out for my recovery). Some days we chatted a lot, and some days we walked in silence. Some days it was fun, and some days it was just necessary. There are a lot of parallels I can talk about, but I want to focus on this: God walks with us. He is with us on the sunny days, but also in the worst snowstorms. Just like with my mum, some days we talk a lot in prayer and feel close to God, and sometimes there are just tears. But he understands it all, the heights of joy and the depths of suffering and grief. My mum and I walked for 200 days in total, continuing until just before Jacob arrived in Canada. But we get to walk with Jesus every day. It's not an easy walk, but even when we can't see him in the middle of a snowstorm, he is still there.

God did not want me to get cancer. He did not want me to go through what I went through. But he used the circumstances of hurting people and a sinful world to bring glory to himself, and to draw Jacob and me closer to Jesus. By the time we were married, I had amassed a large following on social media. I invited everyone to watch the livestream of our wedding, and hundreds of people tuned in live, with the video gaining thousands of views over time. The strongest message in the service was that God is good, that Jesus came to save us, and that his love sustains us. Our testimony was seen by news media, journalists, politicians, family, friends and strangers. As I wept through my vows, I was reminded that this is just the beginning of our story. God has a lot left to come, and we have a powerful testimony that one day we can tell our children and our children's children. Our love story has been a gift, and God has used it in ways that I will never fully understand.

One evening, after my surgery but before we received exemptions, I went for a walk. Headphones in, my finger hovered over a sad song when I felt the Lord tell me not to listen to it. He told me to put on a joyful song and dance. "I'm so sad, the last thing I feel like is dancing," was my response. The impression remained. So I clicked on an old Beach Boys song, and as soon as the notes hit my ears, a massive smile broke out on my face. I walked around the block, dancing and twirling and skipping around. There are gifts, small moments that God gave me like this in the middle of my valley of suffering, that reminded me that he loves me and that he gives joy in all circumstances.

God taught me a lot about trust in him and his plan during this season. He showed me what it means to let go of my plans and submit to his, to live out that surrender every day, over and over again. But the greater lesson was this: he showed me that there is a great privilege in suffering. He doesn't want us to suffer, but we live in a sinful and broken world in which he uses suffering to bring us closer to Jesus and the cross. It brings us to our knees in pain and anguish, but Jesus is right beside us in it, and he understands better than anyone.

When we enter the Lord's presence, there will be no pain, suffering, tears or cancer. This means that while we are on earth we have the unique opportunity to sit in our pain and still choose God. We will never get to choose him and declare his goodness and faithfulness in the same way once we are with him in eternity. Right here in the midst of your deepest suffering, you have the ability to say boldly and defiantly that *God is still good.*

I can think of no greater act of worship than this.

Sarah Taylor is the author's daughter. She lives in Newcastle, England with her husband Jacob.

CHAPTER 2

ROOMS IN THE HOUSE OF GRIEF

Franklin Pyles

This is how the legal story ended.

The man involved in a car crash last June that claimed the life of an Owen Sound-area woman was sentenced Thursday to 75 days in jail and fined $945 for driving while disqualified, refusing to provide police with a breath sample, driving without insurance, driving without proper license plates and failing to appear in court. P H, 44, was charged after the June 8 crash in Owen Sound that killed Anna Pyles, 24, of RR 6 Owen Sound.

This is how the pain began.

I was preparing to leave the church office to go into the evening service when the church phone rang and a person from the hospital informed me that two of my children were in ER and I needed to come. My son was in the car but survived the crash with a broken rib and lingering back pain, but we lost Anna who was the driver.

Anna had been in the Maritimes but a broken relationship brought her back to us pregnant and sorrowing. Through the months of her pregnancy our entire family and our entire church renewed our love for each other and there was strength and hope when her baby girl was born. Three weeks later she was gone from us.

Then the story was repeated, with variations.

My son James was a third year student at Wheaton College when he was instructed by God in a dream to be a missionary to the Arab people of Palestine. He immediately began preparation. He read books, persuaded a teacher to teach his Arabic as a special study, and asked if he could go to Israel on a mission trip the following summer, which he did. In Israel the intifada was winding down, but our family was still concerned. To be honest I had a deep sense of foreboding about the trip. In a thank you video to our church in Owen Sound James asked for prayer for safety and as he left his mother whispered in his ear a southern farewell, "you come back — hear."

But he did not come back. During his time in Israel James not only made friends he was part of a growing movement of God. A man was healed after the team James was part of prayed for him, a man of the majority religion was about to accept Christ, and James directly challenged a Hamas leader with the Gospel. On a nice day James accompanied one of the national evangelists to find a believer who was quite isolated and encourage him to attend a retreat. On a busy two lane road the driver swung out to pass a truck and was suddenly trapped. The resulting collision left James dead.

People would say to me that they cannot imagine what it must be like, and I say back, do not ever try to imagine such a thing, do not ever allow your mind to explore it.

Having said that, I would like to explore the path of healing, and also comment on what things are not part of the path of healing.

Let us first deal with the idea of closure, the idea that at some point a person who is grieving closes the door and is now whole, well, and is able to function in life as they did before their loss.

In 1969 psychiatrist Elizabeth Kubler-Ross published a study of how cancer patients reacted to a terminal diagnosis. In her book *On Death and Dying* she delineated five stages that people passed through: denial, anger, bargaining, depression, and finally acceptance. Even though this study was about people who were dying, it soon was applied in the popular mind as also applying to people who are grieving for someone who has died, or even grieving for almost anything from losing one's job or wallet to breaking up with a boy or girl friend. Thus entered into the public consciousness the concept of closure, the idea that, after a loss, at some point a person can be finished, they have accepted what has happened, they no longer are filled with sorrow, they move on.

It is my opinion that this concept of closure, which is not based on any studies, is false and in fact can do harm to people because they sense an expectation from their community, be it family, church or circle of friends, that their intense feelings of grief and sorrow are an indication of a flaw in their own mental and spiritual health. Certainly we get over a lost wallet, and usually we find a new job and hopefully a new friend, but some losses are profound, they are not the same and should not be lumped in with the minor bumps along life's road. For these profound loses that have wounded the heart the concept of closure may create an excuse among members of the grieving person's community to discontinue support, help and sympathy, all of which are needed for a long time, perhaps for years.

There is in fact no such thing as closure in profound grief. Over time the pain lessens, and every person develops ways and means for continuing life. All of this is natural and necessary. But the wound of loss remains until the day when all tears are washed away, which is the true moment of closure. I am thankful for those friends who did not assume that after a year or so my wife and I were just fine, that we had reached closure and they could simply forget us. These friends continued to remind us that they remembered our children. Over the years they have told us stories, some touching, some humorous, that we had never heard, stories that helped us to remember and appreciate them while acknowledging the immensity of loss. And some of them continued to send cards and sometimes flowers, enabling us to tangibly understand that we were still part of an understanding and loving community.

Instead of looking for closure I would suggest that grief is like a house with a number of rooms. Each room is a possibility and almost every grieving person visits one room or the other at some point in their journey. But eventually one room is picked as the favorite; one room more than others becomes the dwelling place.

DESPAIR

Despair is the dark room without windows. To stay in this room is to slowly shrivel, to lose joy and laughter, to find life worthless.

What is the first question people tend to ask a person who is grieving? "How are you doing?" And what is the answer? It may be "not real well but I will make it through," or even, "I thank the Lord for his strength," or some other answer that is meant to reassure the well-meaning friend. In reality, however, the person may well be teetering on the edge of abject despair, a despair so dark that the body is affected. George Bowering and Jean Baird have edited a book titled *The Heart Does Break*. It does indeed. Numerous people die within a few years of a loss, and may even lose their firm grip on reality. They turn to prescription drugs to mask the pain, or to alcohol, they allow themselves to be filled with fantasies of revenge or, on the opposite end, they may be filled with guilt for not having been able to prevent the tragic course of events and then seek to turn that guilt from themselves by blaming someone else, as I will speak of below. Despair becomes a fertile bed for the growing of a number of poisons, the most lethal being a loss of faith.

Sometimes it seems hard to leave despair because it seems that if we do that leaving is a sign that we did not truly value the person who is gone. Actually it is the opposite.

A person tempted by this room needs to ask a basic question. If life is so joyless, so bleak, so worthless, why should I be sad that the person I loved has left it? Instead, is not my very grief a sign that life is in fact worthwhile, a joy, a value beyond compare, and the fact that I am still here means that I am intended to live it. It is by fully living life that we most strongly signify the value of the person we have lost. Counter-intuitive as it may be, it is true.

BLAME

Someone has died, but why? Someone is dead, so someone must be to blame, for only in finding the one who is to blame can the answer to the question "Why" be found. Or so it may seem. But who is it that is to blame? And, when found, what should be done about it?

The first person that is looked at may be the person who is closest, the other parent if a child has died, or another family member. And this is not kept secret, for the room of blame is a noisy room filled with shouts of recrimination. "I didn't want her to go but you insisted." "You were supposed to check on him, why didn't you?" Slowly, methodically, the event is examined with layer upon layer being peeled back so that at the bottom, so it is thought, it can be firmly established that this or that person is ultimately to blame.

And then what? In many instances where a child dies the one who is blamed is the other parent. For this reason it is believed that among married couples who experience the death of a child, fifty percent divorce with four years of the child's death.

Finding who to blame can also drive a person to seek revenge, or to look to the law to enact revenge. It is a story as old as humanity, for in tribal societies if a person dies there was no judicial system and so it fell to certain family members to go out, find the person who caused the death and exact revenge, that is, kill them. Even today many societies still operate with this system.

In the west we rely on the justice system, but for those who are living in the room of blame it may be mistakenly thought that once the justice system runs its course and the person who is to blame is caught, tried and convicted, that they will then be released, they will at last have closure. But there is no healing in revenge, and while justice must and should be allowed to run its course, it will never bring closure to those whose loss is beyond words.

Looking for others to blame and thinking that when they are either punished or removed from one's life, as in divorce, that peace will come, is thinking that corrodes the spirit. But none of this harms the spirit as much as blaming oneself.

In many situations where a death has been traumatic, well-meaning people will tell the grieving person not to blame themselves, but it may be that there is reason to blame oneself, that true and honest examination reveals the truth that wrong or even improper decisions were made, and a deep and honest self-examination yields the truth that decisions arose from inner orientations or attitudes that were corrupt. Pride, anger, resentment, lack of faith, lack of diligence, and more stare at the grieving person, and what is to be done with that?

I faced all of these options, but the Lord instructed me that absolutely nothing would be helped through blame, for in reality blame is simply part of the terrible room of despair. True, the circumstances of both deaths could easily have been different, so different that the deaths would not have happened. But how many times in life have circumstances been different? That is, how many times have I arrived at an intersection which, if I had arrived a few seconds earlier, or later, there might have been a terrible crash? Life if full of "what ifs" and so, even though there is blame, it is not ours to lay the charge.

This became a particularly pressing issue for us in the death of our son who was a passenger. The driver had acted both foolishly and illegally, but what would be our response? We decided as a family that we all make driving mistakes and that nothing would be gained by seeking to ruin this man's life, a man who was in fact my son's friend and mentor. We went to Israel and not only received him but sought to make him a friend of our family as well. When the government put him on trial I wrote the judge in Israel a letter asking for mercy for him, and because that letter came from me, the father, much mercy was granted. We are so grateful to the Lord, for we believe that a door was opened for the gospel to grow.

Blaming others and blaming oneself may seem like healthy responses because on the surface it appears that finding the right person to blame will answer the final question, "Why did this happen?" But it is not just another person, be it a spouse or the perpetrator, or even ourselves that we are tempted to blame. Ultimately we are tempted to blame God, for no answer to the question "Why" is ever complete without God.

What role did God play in this event which has so torn the heart? This is a question that is found in the first pages of the Bible, when Adam blames God for giving him a wife who would tempt him, and which reverberates all the way through, climaxing at the cross and continuing to the last few pages of promise, this question, why should an evil thing be allowed?

This is not the place to explore, even in a brief manner, the great mystery of God's relation to the events of our lives and of history, a topic that is called the providence of God. What we should look at instead is anger, not mere disappointment but anger at God, for when people are angry with God it is usually not because of God's providence, it is because they had expectations of God that were not met. They expected that in this world of torment and chaos that they would be spared, that being a Christian meant that they and their family would never be caught in storms, buried under buildings that collapse, infected with a disease that suddenly appears in the community, or crushed inside of an automobile. They expected that God would protect them from all of it all of the time. And so they are beyond disappointment, they are enraged. They stop coming to church, the one place where community should sustain them, their prayer life shrivels, and as they slowly grow alienated from Christ and the family of faith the energy of their lives shrinks.
Furious anger soon takes over the room of blame. It darkens. Screams and moaning echo from the walls, and as the room expands to fill the whole heart it becomes dry, empty and barren, a room where there is only hurt and never healing. Flee this room, for only destruction awaits you. Flee into a room where you can be healed.

HOPE

Hope is the room with windows that see tomorrow, that see the resurrection and through which we can view eternity. It is a room full of light, a light so pure that the reality of our loss is always seen vividly with no denial or diminution, but seen in the light of grace.

For some this room is entered by laying hold of the providence of God. God had a purpose. I will be quiet before the will of God. In the end this is true, but while it can generate acceptance it also can push a person towards anger with God, and this anger is not acceptable. Anger with God is not acceptable, not simply because we must be submissive, which we must be, but because it demonstrates a refusal to believe in the purpose of God as shown to us in Jesus Christ.

As our family gathered for a private time to view my son's body, the one glimpse we would allow ourselves, one of my children simply said, "This is why Christ came." If our world was all sweetness, if there was not violence in nature, no evil in people's hearts, no foolishness in their actions, then Jesus would not have needed to come, for a sinless world does not need a Savior. Later I would repeat what my son said with a closer focus, "This is why Christ rose from the dead."

To have hope is to believe in Jesus Christ who came to us, born of a virgin, who suffered under Pontius Pilate, was crucified, buried, and on the third day rose again, who ascended into heaven from which he will come again. To hope is to say, "I believe in the resurrection of the dead and the life everlasting."

In this life we never leave the house of grief, but we do choose which room to live in. I believe that choice is intentional and conscious. I wrote this by hand in my notebook after my daughter left us.

I am here at Wheaton College listening to papers on C. S. Lewis, and constantly thinking of Anna. I began the day offering thanks for her life. She brought to me lightness and laughter. She drew me from my seriousness, and in her shortcomings, revealed to me my sin and my personal failures as a father.

Today, Gilbert Meilaender read a wonderful paper in which he talked about how Lewis brought out that our love for things in this world can — will — become a competition for our love for God. There is pain, severe pain, as God brings us back to himself.

I am in the furnace of this pain. Nothing in my life has made me so aware of my sin as her death. People tell you not to have recriminations against yourself. But I do, because the sins are real. Ultimately, I have been plunged into this pain because I needed and deserved it.

But did she? I cannot comment on that. Instead I know that while what God wills to inflict on me is right and good, the taking of Anna was a robbery. God hated it, it was evil. To say otherwise is to be drawn to a despair from which there is no escape. Here is what comforts me. God hates what happened to my daughter and came to earth in Jesus Christ to rescue her. Because of Christ she lives, and will be raised again.

So, I turn with love to God, not a God who hurts me — although I am hurt — but the God who loved her and at enormous cost rescued her.

On Palm Sunday night I left three palms, which I lifted from the communion table, on her grave. For the first time I felt the defiant hope of the resurrection. I shouted, "I'll see you again."

It hurts so much — but I am seeking to learn patience and hope of seeing Christ who saved me, and her. Thank you.

Dr Franklin Pyles is the past president of the Christian and Missionary Alliance in Canada. He and his wife Gay are now retired and live in Wisconsin.

CHAPTER 3

PUTTING THE FOUNDATIONS IN PLACE

When my friends Franklin and Gay Pyles buried their daughter Anna, I was there. And, a few years later, when they buried their son James. How do I respond to what Franklin has written? The best way to start is probably remembering how I stood singing a hymn during Anna's service. In fact, I remember the hymn. It was "Praise my soul, the king of heaven." And I remember looking to the front row, where Franklin had his hands raised in praise. And I remember beginning to weep. The hymn builds to a crescendo in the final stanza:

Frail as summer's flower we flourish,
Blows the wind and it is gone;
But while mortals rise and perish
God endures unchanging on,
Praise Him, praise Him,
Praise Him, praise Him,
Praise the High Eternal One!

And in the midst of the incredible grief born of the knowledge that the wind had indeed passed over one we love and they are gone, God gave grace to my friends to live out the command of the last three lines of the hymn.

And I remember more. I remember speaking with Franklin in the receiving line some years later when his son James died. I remember being in tears again. I remember sharing with Franklin my realization that God might take one of my kids. And I remember him telling me to plead the blood of Jesus over each one of them. And I remember in the service those hands once again raised in praise.

Perhaps after reading the previous chapter, you have a deeper understanding of how Franklin and Gay found the strength to praise God in the midst of the most awful and humanly inexplicable suffering.

No one can fully explain the fact of human suffering any more than they can fully illuminate the meaning of the Trinity or the interrelationship between God's sovereignty and human free will. Our human minds are simply not capable of such tasks. But that does not mean we cannot try. It does not mean we cannot understand better than we have ever done before. Understand well enough to be able to help ourselves and others grapple with suffering and come through it with a real measure of healing.

This is a book about suffering. But more than that, it is a book about God and his ways. To understand suffering, or any human experience, requires first an understanding of God. The key to understanding what happens in God's creation is understanding the Creator himself. Everything we are going to say is based on the following basic truths about God as revealed in the Bible.

GOD HAS AUTHORITY OVER ALL THINGS

The Bible begins with these words, "In the beginning, God created the heavens and the earth" (Gen. 1:1). It then adds the detail, "And the Spirit of God was hovering over the face of the waters" (Gen. 1:2). The New Testament shows us the Son was there also, "In the beginning was the Word, and the Word was with God, and the Word was God. He was in the beginning with God. All things were made through him, and without him was not anything made that was made" (Jn. 1:1-3). Paul expands on this, "For by him all things were created.... all things were created through him and for him. And he is before all things, and in him all things hold together" (Col. 1:16-17). God created the world, and he sustains the world. The last book of the Bible completes the story. The same God who created the world will one day eradicate the evil that invaded it and restore his perfect creation. The garden temple in which Adam and Eve dwelt as priests will be restored in the temple of the new Jerusalem. The only difference is that evil will never be allowed inside its gates. Revelation presents God as "the Alpha and the Omega... who is and who was and who is to come" (Rev. 1:8). The meaning of this declaration is that God is Lord over the beginning of history, over the end of history and over everything in between.

GOD HAS AUTHORITY OVER THE LIVES OF BELIEVERS

Paul states boldly that God is sovereign over the lives of his people, "And we know that for those who love God all things work together for good, for those who are called according to his purpose. For those whom he foreknew he also predestined to be conformed to the image of his Son..." (Rom. 8:28). A key in understanding these words is to realize that the "all things" that God works together for good is a reference to the "sufferings of this present time" of verse 18. It is not when things are easy that we need to know God is sovereign, but when they are hard. In times of crisis, the early Christians reminded themselves that even the circumstances of Jesus' death expressed nothing more nor less than what God had "predestined to take place" (Ac. 4:28). God chose us before the foundation of the world, and he "predestined us for adoption as sons and daughters through Jesus Christ" (Eph. 1:4-5).

GOD HAS AUTHORITY OVER SATAN

One of the most fascinating things about the last book of the Bible is the way in which it describes the authority of God over Satan. Satan is thrown down to earth when he challenges God's authority by trying to destroy Christ (Rev. 12:4). War breaks out in heaven. As Christ is resurrected from the dead, Satan is cast out of heaven, and his place of accusation against believers is destroyed (12:7-12). He is then thrown into a prison and bound with a great chain for a thousand years (20:1-2). The thousand years is a figurative way of describing the period from Christ's resurrection until his return. During this time, his powers to deceive are so restricted that he cannot stop the movement of the kingdom of God across the earth (20:3). At the end of history, God allows him to be released (20:3), and the church briefly appears defeated (11:7-10). God himself superintends the gathering together of the pagan nations under Satan's command (16:12-16; 19:19; 20:8-9), but only in order to bring them all to final destruction (19:20-21; 20:10).

This interaction between God and Satan is worked out in miniature in a situation in Paul's life. He is afflicted by a thorn in the flesh, a "messenger of Satan" (2 Cor. 12:7). Yet this messenger was released into Paul's life by God, whose sovereign purpose was to use his suffering to eradicate pride in the apostle's life, "so to keep me from becoming conceited," a phrase repeated at the beginning and end of the verse.

Satan has power, but only as much power as God allows ultimately for his own purposes. Satan is not omniscient — he does not know what God alone knows. That is precisely why Satan had Jesus nailed to the cross without realizing that in that very act he was bringing about the ultimate failure of his own purposes. God has authority over sinful people

If God is sovereign over the devil, he is sovereign over those who follow the enemy. Few people had their lives so apparently ruined than Joseph had, and by the members of his own family. Being torn away from his loving father and sold into slavery was bad enough. But then he was thrown into prison because of his refusal to dishonor his master, and then falsely blamed for doing the opposite. Finally, after the amazing revelation he had in prison to the king's servant, the butler forgot his promise to speak to Pharaoh on Joseph's behalf, and he remained in prison two more long years. Why? Because God was fashioning a plan to use the weather systems of the ancient world to his own ends, and that plan had to await its fulfillment. At the end of it all, when Joseph's family was restored to him, he was able to make this statement to his brothers who had so badly wronged him, "As for you, you meant evil against me, but God meant it for good" (Gen. 50:20).

Even Judas was raised up by the foreknowledge and counsel of God. Jesus said he had lost none of those entrusted to him except for the "son of destruction, that the Scripture might be fulfilled" (Jn. 17:12). The mob arresting Jesus was sent only in order that "the Scriptures be fulfilled" (Mt. 26:54). God raised up Herod, Pilate, and the Gentiles and Jews who crucified Jesus by the plan he himself had determined (Ac. 5:27-28).

GOD CALLS US TO REMEMBER HIS FAITHFULNESS IN TIMES OF TROUBLE

The question we have to face with suffering is not the reality of God's sovereignty, or his love or faithfulness toward us. The question is what our response will be to what we are going through. Will we respond with a trust which opens the way for God to do whatever he wants with us? Or will we respond in bitterness or anger, which will close the door to his work in us? Much of this depends on how well we have learned to see the hand of God in our lives. God told Moses to instruct the Israelites to recite the story of their deliverance from Egypt to each generation so they would never forget his mighty works and faithfulness. When they first left Egypt, Moses said this, "Remember this day in which you came out from Egypt, out of the house of slavery, for by a strong hand the Lord brought you out from this place" (Exod. 13:3). And when they were about to enter the Promised Land forty years later, he repeated his message, "You shall remember that you were a slave in the land of Egypt, and the Lord your God brought you out from there with a mighty hand and an outstretched arm" (Deut. 5:15). When they faced an apparently invincible enemy, they were to remember again what God had done for them, "If you say in your heart, 'These nations are greater than I. How can I dispossess them?' you shall not be afraid of them but you shall remember what the Lord your God did to Pharaoh and to all Egypt" (Deut. 7:17-18). The Hebrew verb for "remember" (*zakar*), used in all these passages, means a remembering which results in action. For people to *remember* the commandments means for them to *obey* the commandments, "So you shall remember and do all my commandments, and be holy to your God" (Num. 15:40). Remembering the great works of God and his acts of faithfulness gave the Israelites a framework or perspective, a way of seeing and understanding things, especially in the midst of hardship or battle. The same God who delivered them in that battle would rescue them again. This was never to be forgotten by them, and was to provide a framework for their understanding of God. We also need to learn to recite the good things of God, how he has delivered us and helped us in the past, and to remember his goodness toward us. When we remember, we take the appropriate action associated with the remembering, which is to trust God for the present trial and continue to act in obedience toward him, in view of his faithfulness in times and trials past. When trouble approaches, we have a framework of God's faithfulness through which to look at it, instead of simply panicking and falling apart.

GOD CALLS US TO SEE THINGS WITH HIS VISION

The error of the Israelites was they saw only what was physically around them. They saw Pharaoh's army behind them and the Red Sea in front of them. They saw a desert with no water. They saw a wilderness with no food. Yet God parted the sea, destroyed the army, gave water through the rock, and rained down manna from heaven. But still they did not learn. They saw giants bigger than them, and lost heart. They chose to minimize God and his faithfulness and the great works he had done, of which they were well aware, and they chose to maximize the works and the power of the enemy instead. Satan will always try to intimidate us in the same way, making himself appear greater than us or God. That is why the Bible addresses us with these words, "He who is in you is greater than he who is in the world" (1 Jn. 4:4).

We need to learn to see differently. In 2 Cor. 4:17-18, Paul makes an amazing statement about the sovereignty of God in suffering. He teaches us how, through seeing things correctly, we can make it through those times. Listen to him speak, "For this light momentary affliction is preparing for us an eternal weight of glory beyond all comparison, as we look [*skopeo*] not to the things that are seen [*blepo*] but to the things that are unseen. For the things that are seen are transient, but the things that are unseen are eternal." The first word for seeing (translated "look") is *skopeo*, and means to gaze intently at something, as if we were looking through the "scope" of a rifle. *This way we can see things which cannot be seen by natural vision.* The second word (*blepo*) is the ordinary Greek word for seeing. There are two types of sight. One is natural and the other is supernatural. Two people can pass through the same set of events and evaluate them completely differently. *Only those who begin to see by supernatural vision what God is doing through the events can make the right responses and grow from what they are going through.* Others will have various unfortunate responses. They may see themselves as helpless victims of fate. They may ignore issues in their lives that contributed to their problems. They may think God is punishing them for some known or unknown sin. Or perhaps just that God has somehow forgotten about them. These people are candidates for bitterness and self-pity. Not infrequently, they damage themselves by wrong or mistaken responses more than they were affected by the original issue.

This is not what God wants for us. Christians should refuse to look only at what can be seen with the natural eye. Instead, we should choose to fix our sights on the things which cannot be seen naturally, things which cannot be seen with ordinary vision, but only with the supernatural vision that God himself gives. This supernatural vision is birthed out of remembering his past faithfulness to us, starting with our salvation and deliverance from eternal judgment, and continuing in a thousand ways right up to the present. It is in a very real sense focussed on the eternal world, not the visible world in front of us. Only through this kind of vision can we understand and respond to suffering in the way God wants, and to see him accomplish his purposes in the midst of it.

GOD HAS A PLAN

God has a plan he is working out in the midst of our suffering. Our trials are not random events outside of his control. Where the enemy has attacked us and caused us harm and pain, our first priority should be to know how to work with God in it. What is he teaching us? Why has he allowed us to go through this? How is he refining us? In what ways is he drawing us closer to himself? Is he dealing with wrong dependencies on people or things other than himself? Are there areas of disobedience in which we have opened ourselves to attack? Maybe, as with Joseph, there is a greater plan involving more than just our individual lives, in which our testing is part of something wider God is preparing.

God is not the source of suffering. Our rebellion, which allowed sin and death into the world, is leveraged by Satan for his purposes, and that is the culprit. However, God uses even the plans of the enemy for good. Suffering becomes the occasion of God's discipline, or even an opportunity for a deeper understanding and receiving of God's love. God's discipline is not punishment. It is a loving drawing of us toward him through his teaching us and holding us in adversity. Though painful, it is always for our good (Heb. 12:5-11). It yields the "peaceful fruit of righteousness to those who have been trained by it" (Heb. 12:11). It brings peace with God, maturity and fruitfulness in God's service.

Often we put up walls and hide behind them, because we are afraid of a greater demand of God on our lives or families. God graciously uses suffering to tear down those walls. *His goal is to make us more fearful of disobeying him than of any possible personal challenges.* Other times we are just scared of going through things because we don't really have the assurance that God will show up for us. God will use trials to enable us to discover that he does keep us in the midst of them. Overcoming fear through suffering is often the beginning of our usefulness for God.

Olympic athletes risk injury because they seek something worth the risk —the chance for gold. They learn from their injuries. They take better care of their bodies. They study how to perform more professionally. They train harder. They know their limits, but they do not give up, walk away or consider themselves the victim of circumstances. How much more should this be so with Christians who strive for the greatest prize of all, and who know and are convinced of the reality of a God who cares for them and who is working all things together for good for those who love him?

It can be hard, especially when times are tough, to discern what God is doing. But with a right heart, solid friends around us and lots of prayer, and sometimes after the dust has settled a little, we can usually begin to see his hand at work. How many times have we looked back and said something like this, "I wouldn't want to go through that again, but I am glad somehow that it happened. Because of what God did in me and taught me, I am stronger, not weaker, because of it." Maybe we had an accident. We were hurt, but not killed. We saw not how God abandoned us, but how he protected us. Maybe a relationship broke down, but it turned out to be a relationship that needed to break down. Maybe we went bankrupt, but God taught us how to handle money and possessions differently as a result. Maybe we lost a job, but it turned out God gave us a better one.

Or maybe a truly inexplicable tragedy happened. We lost a child. Our spouse walked out and never came back. We contracted a debilitating illness from which there is no cure. Sometimes tragedies happen which we will never fully understand in this life. Some of these are written about in this book. We do live in a fallen world. We are all exposed in some measure to the effects of sin. Bad things happen to God's people. But God is there in it all. He has not abandoned us. It is not easy to do, but with his help we can begin to see into an eternal realm where what happens in this life is less significant than what happens in the next, where death for the believer is the glorious and triumphant entrance into true life.

We are a people who should be able to see something greater, who have access to a deeper knowledge and understanding, who can find gold in the rubble of life, who can receive strength not only for ourselves but for others, who can face the giants and go in and possess the land. These are the kind of people God will use to extend his kingdom. We don't have to be rich, clever or gifted in any way, but we do need to be men and women who have experienced the faithfulness of God in the struggles of life, and are still standing in faithful response to him. We need to be people who can see what others cannot see, and who are confident not in their own ability, but in God's ability. We need to be people who seek his kingdom, no matter what the cost.

Mary Magdalene's life changed forever the moment she cried out the words that heralded the greatest event in history, "I have seen the Lord!" (Jn. 20:18). As we begin to see him and his plan for us more clearly, it will change our lives too. I hope this book will help you to that end.

REFLECTIONS FOR DISCUSSION:

How do you see the interaction between the sovereignty of God and the presence of evil in the world? How is it that God can remain holy and yet allow both Satan and sinful people to operate in disobedience to him? What is the higher purpose God is achieving through all this?

Have you learned something new in this chapter about the Biblical concept of remembering? How can you put it into effect in your life?

What is the idea of having spiritual vision so significant for the believer and how have you seen this play out in your own walk with the Lord?

CHAPTER 4

PATHWAY TO HOPE

Paul addresses the issue of suffering head-on in these five verses, "Therefore, since we have been justified by faith, we have peace with God through our Lord Jesus Christ. Through him we have also obtained access by faith into this grace in which we stand, and we rejoice in the hope of the glory of God. Not only that, but we rejoice in our sufferings, knowing that suffering produces endurance, and endurance produces character, and character produces hope, and hope does not put us to shame, because God's love has been poured into our hearts through the Holy Spirit whom has been given us to us" (Rom. 5:1-5).

Rejoicing in hope is one thing, but to rejoice in suffering? Here is where the Gospel message hits the hard wall of our selfishness. One or the other must give way. And the result of that battle will determine the course of our lives and our effectiveness for God. *The issue is not whether suffering will come, but how we deal with it when it does come.* And that is what this Scripture addresses.

God has a pathway to hope. But this pathway not does not lead the way we would have expected — through fields of blessing and prosperity. Rather, it leads through narrow paths of trial and difficulty. Yet Paul says here that in the end, it is the only way we can find true hope. Several chapters later, he says that God has a plan to turn everything for good in the lives of those who love him (Rom. 8:28). This passage shows us how he intends to do this.

God is not a sadist. He does not command us to want suffering in our lives. But he is telling us that when suffering comes, as it will, he will give us the ability to rejoice in the midst of it. Let's watch as he develops his argument.

He starts with this one foundational fact: we have been justified by faith (verse 1). Jesus has taken the punishment for our sin on his sinless shoulders. As a result, we have peace with God. We are now his friends, no longer his enemies. Because of that, we now have access to his presence. The word used for "access" refers to the right to enter a king's throne room.

Of course, just because we have the right does not mean that the right is automatically exercised. It remains *our choice* whether or not to enter into the throne room of the King. The throne room is the place of relationship, the place where we meet God, the place of prayer, of fellowship with him. It is not populated only by saintly people who spend hours every day on their knees. It also includes the dad on the way to work coming into God's presence in his car and lifting his day and his family before the Lord. It includes the mom who has just sent her kids off to school, quickly asking the Father's blessing and protection on them as they go. It includes the student anxious before an important exam asking God for help. It includes the employee worried about her job and asking the Lord to help her as she makes her way to work. That's what it means to enter God's throne room. That throne room is the only place on earth you will find the grace of God. If you want its benefits, you have to make the decision to enter.

What is the grace of God that we access in this throne room? The grace of God is the strength that God provides for us to live life abundantly. It is the strength drawn from the infinite resources of the Creator. It is the power by which the universe was created, and the power by which it is still moment by moment held together. Wouldn't you rather live by that strength than by whatever resources you can find within yourself? In his mercy, God brings us to the end of our strength so that we can find his strength instead. Letting go of our tiny security blankets enables us to fall into the security only he can provide. The grace is there for our asking, but we must ask, "You do not have, because you do not ask" (Jas. 4:2). It does not come automatically. But because God has done all this for us we can find strength, by the grace he alone provides, no matter what the circumstances.

How a Christian faces suffering should be radically different from the attitude of a non-believer. For the Christian, suffering leads first to endurance (verse 3). Endurance is the determination to focus on the goodness and character of God when trouble comes. As Paul says elsewhere, "Give thanks in all circumstances" (1 Thess. 5:18). Endurance chooses to remember that the faithfulness and eternal reward of God outweigh any present and temporary suffering. It gives us God's perspective on what is happening to us. It's what saves us from becoming embittered at God and others. I remember watching news reports of people being rescued from a natural catastrophe. Many were very bitter, and even cursed those who came to help them. But some who were Christians were praising the Lord for their deliverance, even though they had suffered just as much as the others. Which people came out of that situation with peace in their hearts and equipped to pick up the pieces and begin to rebuild? Which ones came out scarred and even more bitter than before? Endurance is the willingness to keep on in the midst of trial with a good heart and attitude, looking to God and praising him for his goodness. God is not looking for perfection before he responds to us. Without doubt, each of us passes through times of darkness, despair and anger, yet in Christ we find the strength to make our way through it while still trusting him.

The second step in the pathway to hope comes as endurance leads on to character (verse 4a). The word "character" refers to the testedness of a metal which is refined in the fire and comes through pure. Peter compares this process of testing metal to the refining of our faith through times of trial (1 Pet. 1:7). A tested character is a character with substance. Have you ever met people who seem to have little substance once you scratch the surface of who they are? Continued perseverance and faithfulness to God produces an ever-deepening relationship with Christ and dependency on him, which brings an ever-increasing flow of his strength and grace into our lives. As this flow continues, it gives our lives substance. Hebrews 1:3 tells us that Christ is the exact representation of God's substance. "Substance" was a word originally used to refer to sediment, and came to mean something immoveable, as in a rock-solid foundation. Heb. 11:1 tells us that our faith in Christ is the substance of the things hoped for but not yet possessed. The pathway to hope is built on the substance or rock-solid foundation of Christ. He creates in us a faith which itself is like a rock under our feet. This strong and unshakeable foundation is sturdy enough for us to build our lives on *in the midst of suffering*, and even take on the burdens of others. Thus, we become people of real character and substance.

The third step in this pathway out of suffering and into hope is where character leads on to hope (verse 4b). Now we have foundations in our lives that were never there before. As the tides of adversity rise, we find that we are able to cope with things that would have stressed, weakened or even devastated us before. Can you look back at your life and see how things you are now able to deal with would have been very difficult for you five years ago? As we realize what God has done in building solid foundations which cannot be shaken, hope arises in our hearts. Hope shows us how God has continually turned bad situations around for good. Hope looks to the future. Hope is ultimately directed toward our certain victory at the Lord's return, yet it also assures us that, whatever we have yet to face, the Lord will be with us and take us through it. Hope assures us that we will emerge ever stronger at the end, though we may still have to go through difficult times. Hope encourages us that God has a plan for our lives, and that he will never leave us until he has brought us through safely to his heavenly kingdom (2 Tim. 4:18). *Hope is what keeps us until deliverance comes.*

And this leads us to the last step. This hope does not put us to shame because God's love is poured out through his Spirit into our hearts (verse 5). God backs up this hope with his presence and the reality of his love. In the Old Testament, the verb "pour out" is used more often of the pouring out of God's wrath. But now in this present age, through Christ's sacrifice for us, his love instead has been poured out upon us. Paul could have said simply that God's love was *given to us.* But he chose to use a much more powerful word. His love has been *lavished upon us.*

The knowledge of God's love is the guaranteed inheritance of every believer who is willing to take hold of it. This knowledge is not just intellectual but experiential. In the throne room of God's presence, we find an assurance of his love for us. We find a promise that he will never leave us or forsake us. We find him speaking to our mind, our will and our emotions. We find him, as John Wesley put it, "strangely warming" our hearts. This love floods the innermost parts of our being with strength and confidence. It turns our mourning into dancing. It puts our sorrows into perspective. It gives us hope, for the very reason that we know we have a God who holds our future in his hands and will look after us, no matter what. This hope does not put us to shame, because it is fortified, strengthened and empowered by the supernatural knowledge and experience of the Father's amazing, incredible, supernatural love. This is the same experience David had of finding the Father's love in the midst of adversity, "Therefore let everyone who is godly offer prayer to you at a time when you may be found; surely in the rush of great waters, they shall not reach him. You are a hiding place for me; you preserve me from trouble; you surround me with shouts of deliverance... Many are the sorrows of the wicked, but steadfast love surrounds the one who trusts in the Lord. Be glad in the Lord, and rejoice, O righteous, and shout for joy, all you upright in heart!" (Ps. 32:6-7, 10-11).

Sometimes it is suggested that the experience of God's love is easier for a woman to grasp than a man. There is no doubt in my mind that women are more naturally relational than men and perhaps in a better position to take hold of the meaning of God's love. Men are understandably turned off by phrases like "falling in love with Jesus." But here, Paul clearly teaches we receive this love straight from the Father. Every man can identify with the need to have a father's affirmation and approval. Few boys ever lived who could live happily without it, and men who have never had the affirmation and love of a father constitute a major source of family breakdown. But as Christians, we have found the answer for men as well as for women! We can reconnect with the Father who created us. His love is an affirmation, an approval. It is the Father's heart to draw us, men and women alike, into relationship with him.

Engineers learned a powerful lesson from the flooding of New Orleans in the hurricane of 2005. In days before the city was settled, the floodwaters of the Mississippi River from time to time rolled over the floodplain where the city is now located. Every time this happened, the receding waters left behind deposits of silt from the riverbed. Over the centuries, these deposits or sediment built up the areas which are now the high ground of the city. Not only that, outlying ridges of high ground and islands were established which provided additional defences. When the city was settled, originally only the high ground was built on. In later years, engineers built up the levies or dikes in order that lower areas could be inhabited. But the unintended effect of these levies was that, in the process of keeping out those Mississippi floodwaters, they also kept out the deposits of sediment. Furthermore, the areas within the city began to sink and the outlying ridges began to recede. In the end, the full force of nature was vented against the man-made dikes and they failed. Interestingly, the original areas of high ground, built up over the centuries, were never flooded.

Now transfer this idea to what we have been saying about suffering. If we equate the floodwaters with suffering, we would see that, in facing suffering with perseverance, we receive the build-up of sediment, the original meaning of the word "substance" in Greek. The sediment represents the substance of faith and tested character God builds through adversity into our lives. It is a strong foundation for our lives. When the floods of suffering come along the next time, we have a higher ground to protect us and get us through. This in turn releases hope within us that in spite of whatever we are going through, God is working out a plan.

What happens when we try to protect ourselves from suffering, when we try to build artificial walls of protection around us just as the people of New Orleans did a century or more ago? Have we adopted an outlook which holds forth the deception that bad things will never happen to us? Have we turned the Gospel into a message of positive thinking? Have we made God into little more than the deliverer of earthly blessings? If so, we will be bitterly disappointed, not to mention completely unprepared when the hard times come. Having no filter by which to understand how God uses suffering, we will waste opportunities to allow him to build the ground higher underneath us.

No one should picture God as deliberately intending to put us through the wringer. God created a perfect world without suffering. We are to blame for its fallenness. But in the fallen world in which we now live, our lives as Christians, in rubbing up against the rebellion of this world, will suffer in our confrontation with it. Not only that, we must all experience the apparent randomness of sickness and suffering which occurs, like nuclear fallout, simply as a result of the presence of sin and evil in the fallen world in which we live.

But what if we asked God to adjust our understanding? What if we could experience suffering from within the bastion of his presence? What if we could grasp suffering from the wider perspective of God's love for us? What if we took for granted that suffering is a part of life, but asked God to use that suffering to build character in our lives? What if we continued to persevere and be faithful to God when those times came? What if we began to enter into real hope as we saw him winning victories in our lives as our foundations become stronger and stronger? If we try to protect ourselves from all suffering, through man-made defences, those defences will fail. We can practice positive thinking. We can believe God will bring us only prosperity and blessing. We can think ourselves immune to all adversity in life. We can choose to be deluded. What if Jesus had decided to protect himself from suffering by calling on the legions of angels instead of submitting to the cross? Where would that leave us? And how can we, as his followers, pursue a different road than he did?

But as God adjusts our thinking, we can see suffering as only a part, and in the end a small part, of a much greater and more wonderful process. He takes us from the flood plains to the high ground. We will triumph in adversity not because we never experience it, but because we have foundations that sustain us in the midst of it. Jesus talked about a house built on rock and another built on sand. He did not say that the storm would hit only the latter. He told us that the rains would fall and the floods would come on both, but only one would survive, because it had solid foundations (Mt. 7:24-27). It had substance.

If we understand this passage correctly, it teaches us not only that suffering and perseverance are the pathway to hope, *but that they are the only pathway.* Remember Jesus said that the way is narrow that leads to life (Mt. 7:14). The important thing to remember is that *it is the way to life.* If we keep the end of the journey in mind, the way will prove much easier to navigate.

And all along the journey, we will know the reality of his presence and his love. The love of God is the greatest force known to humanity. It surmounted all of our rebellion against him. It sent his Son to the cross. And because of it, he has now justified us, given us peace with himself, provided access to his presence, and lavished upon us his grace. It has been poured out into our hearts through his Spirit. The reality of God's love may not answer every question about our suffering or that of others, but it does and always will put those questions into the greater perspective of an eternal God who, in the end, has an inheritance for us in his love which will remain when all suffering is gone.

This is the glory of God.

REFLECTIONS FOR DISCUSSION:

Has reading this chapter given you a new perspective on the meaning and operation of grace in the believer's life? If so, how? Have you experienced grace in this way before?

What does the Biblical concept of hope mean to you and how do you see it relating to the love of God?

Is it really possible to see suffering as a means of building our house on rock and not sand, when so often suffering seems to be so destructive? It's counterintuitive, but is it correct?

CHAPTER 5

THE WOMAN WHO FOUND THE WELL

On June 8, 2004, my husband Mark and I found ourselves at the Breast Clinic of our local hospital. Having had a physical examination, mammogram and biopsy in the morning I had been asked to "grab something to eat and return at 2pm for the results." It is safe to say we were unable to eat anything as we watched the hands on the cafeteria clock slowly tick by. There were only two of us ladies awaiting results and we both sat in silence with our partners. We occasionally glanced over and with unspoken words sent best wishes across the room with looks and tentative smiles.

The other couple were called first and within minutes I could see them coming out of the consultation room beaming, relieved and planning a take-out to celebrate their news! I was called next, and as I stood up to follow the nurse she stopped and politely asked if Mark wanted to join me. At that split second Mark and I locked eyes and in an instant we knew that the outcome was not what we had hoped for. There were to be no celebrations that evening. I had breast cancer and needed surgery immediately. This was not what we had planned for, as we had moved in together some weeks earlier to start a new life as a blended family.

Raised in a Christian home, as a young girl I just wanted the "fairy tale" — a husband, children, possibly my own career, a house and to live the type of life that I saw my parents and grandparents enjoy. Sadly, that is not how life turned out. I could not have predicted that by the time I was in my early forties I would have been married four times with four children from three different fathers, and facing yet another divorce. Each time I got married, I was genuinely in love with my husband and most sincerely meant the words, "till death us do part." What I got each time was heartache and mental and/or physical abuse. Over the years my self-confidence was shattered, dignity lost, and bones physically broken. My faith in God ebbed away. It took my Dad, whom I adored, to be killed in an accident when I was 29 for me to say to God, "We are done!"

I remember returning from burying my Dad. As I fell on my knees sobbing, I started to rip out the pages of the Bible, raging against God.

"Where were you when I was being mentally abused?"
"Why didn't you intervene?"
"Why didn't you protect my kids?"

I knew full well that *I* was the one that had taken the wrong decisions throughout my life and I took responsibility for the fallout that followed, yet I felt totally abandoned by God. This was a God who can raise the dead and give sight to the blind, so why didn't he hear my prayers? Why did he allow me to go through that hell and leave me broken?

So, here I was, 43 years old, having just moved in with Mark and still chasing the dream of finding someone to love me, only to be told I have cancer and if I didn't act now, I would likely be dead in six months. My life could not have been more of a mess.

In due course, I had surgery and embarked on an aggressive chemotherapy treatment which had to be halted after eight rounds instead of twelve. We knew that the cancer had spread through my lymph nodes and that it might return in the future. Chemotherapy was brutal, and there were occasions when I got so sick that Mark was told that had the ambulance not been called when it was I could have died.

But Mark stayed with me. In fact, he married me in the November of that year. He was with me at every appointment and treatment. He helped shave my head, as I was determined my hair would go on my terms and not due to chemotherapy. He held me day after day as I experienced continuous vomiting with the treatment.

During this time, my brother Dave kept inviting me to his church. Mark was not a Christian and could not understand why God would allow this suffering to take place. I had mellowed somewhat over the years, and was at the point where I believed I knew why my life had unraveled as it had. I was four times divorced and now five times married. I had broken my wedding vows repeatedly. I truly believed that I had blown it with God. I felt so sinful, unclean and faithless. I had not only let my parents and family down, I had also let my children down. I felt utterly worthless in God's eyes.

My brother persisted in his invitations, so to shut him up I agreed to go to church that Sunday. As I listened to the singing and saw people with hands raised praising God there was part of me that so wanted to have that relationship with God again, but as far as I was concerned that ship had sailed. The preacher stood up and started to read from John 4, the story of the woman at the well. I knew this passage well and when he read verse 17, "…the fact is you have five husbands…", Mark looked at me and smiled. The whole way home Mark could not stop talking about how friendly people were, how great the music was, and how funny it was that there was someone in the Bible with five husbands like me.

We were invited back some weeks later and once again the sermon, this time delivered by someone else, was on the very same passage. This time I was a bit irritated, as I was sure Dave had told the pastor my story and this was some kind of set-up. But again Mark loved it and wanted to go back. I was definitely not of the same opinion. The next time we were invited I said no, no and no until I found out that it was a family service. Knowing that they would be preaching to the children, I felt safe and so we attended. The pastor walked to the front of the platform. Looking down at the children who sat cross-legged at the front, he explained that he was going to tell them a story about the woman who had five husbands. He had his hand held up counting his fingers that were splayed out. The children gasped and some giggled. I was fuming and had I not been in the middle of a row, I would certainly have got up to leave.

Dave had been invited to our home for lunch afterwards and I was so angry with him, knowing now that this was indeed a set-up. Dave calmly replied that none of leaders in the church knew anything at all about me, but perhaps it was God who knew how I was feeling, and maybe he was speaking directly to me — all I had to do was listen. The next Sunday I recommitted my life to God, and Mark became a Christian. I realized that God had not left my side, he had not forsaken me and he was ready for me with open arms. Once I had brought my hurts, actions, words and anger to the cross, that was it — they were put in a lake that had a 'no fishing' sign up on it!

My chemotherapy and radiotherapy treatment finished in 2005. Mark and I began our journey with God learning about his grace, his forgiveness, his love and the strength he provides for each one of us during difficult times. Everything that happens is known by God and it happens under his supervsion and with a purpose. We don't always know what that purpose is and we don't always appreciate God's timing, but I remembered reading the book "When your world falls apart" by David Jeremiah. In it, he says there is no need for you to be up all night with worry. God already works the night shift. That really taught me to put my worries and concerns in God's hands. He went on to share how Alexander the Great was once asked how he slept so soundly with dangers all around. Alexander replied that his guard watched over him. So how soundly should we sleep with God watching over us?

I am thrilled to say that Mark and I are still together and in love seventeen years later. I have the most amazing husband who loves me, supports me, looks after me and I am so grateful to wake up with him each morning. I have my "fairytale." Yet our life still has bumps in the road. My health suffered a further setback in 2017 when I was diagnosed with acute pancreatitis. Pancreatitis is usually caused by alcohol or gallstones, and so I had my gallbladder removed in 2018 (which was my eighth surgery). As I take a morphine each day I rarely drink and with my gallbladder removed, the doctors were confident that we had resolved the problem. But later in 2018 I had another bout of pancreatitis, and when a further round hit in July 2019, Mark took me straight to the hospital.

I had a number of tests, and then a doctor appeared who introduced herself as a breast specialist. I laughed and said "I'm pancreas, not breast – I think you need someone else." She told me very gently that she was with the right patient, and that the radiologist had found unusual markers on my spine. She believed that my breast cancer had returned, but this time had spread to my bones. "It's stage four," she said. "I am very sorry to tell you but this is not curable, although there are treatments available to extend life."

I was absolutely lost for words. Everything seemed to move in slow motion. I looked at Mark in horror at what she was saying — palliative care, terminal, stage four! This was a nightmare and I couldn't even catch my breath. The doctor left to allow Mark and I to have some time together. We cried, we hugged and then just tried to process what had just been said. It was like a nuclear bomb had just been dropped on us. Would I see my son get married? Would I see my grandchildren finish school? So many questions were racing through our heads.

We consulted the great Dr. Google, which is never a good idea, only to learn that no more than 18% of people with secondary breast cancer and bone metastases make it to five years. The average life expectancy is 18 – 24 months. We both felt this was not news we could give to our six children and other family members over the phone. We phoned David and Elaine, our good friends in Canada. Thankfully they were home and available. Having shared the news, we prayed and shed tears.

Today I am fast approaching my two year post-diagnosis marker. I have taken early retirement so that I can spend my "good hours" and "good days" with my family. We have bought a puppy who has brought so much joy to us both. This was a purposeful purchase so that after I die, Mark cannot lock himself away – he has to get up every morning and take the dog out for walks. We have updated our wills. The Power of Attorney for health, finance and property documentation is completed and filed. We have had conversations with the family about my wishes, turning off the life support machine if appropriate and even agreed where I will die, at home or in a hospice. My funeral has been planned and paid for, so nobody needs to worry about that when the time comes.

As you can tell, I am an organizer and feel so pleased that all of those difficult decisions have already been taken and everything is in place, so that after I die things will be easier for those left behind. They are the "earthly" things I needed to do, and I can rest in the knowledge that in that respect at least Mark is looked after.

So how do I feel right now? I feel confused as to why we are where we are. At times I do privately cry at the thought of leaving Mark behind. I deal with pain every day and night and I live from hospital appointments, CT and MRI scans, one after the other, to mark the progression of my cancer. Cancer has taken so much in terms of my body, my energy, my ability to work, my ability to run, climb/hike, dance and possibly my future.

However I need to remind myself that we all die one day, and at some point we should be prepared for that. Sometimes I feel that the cancer has been a gift. It has brought me back into a relationship with God, which is worth everything. I have found that when in my own strength I am weak is just when Christ in me is strong. God will enable me to do whatever he wants me to do. Just before writing this I was reading Acts 5, where the apostles were flogged by the religious leaders, yet they rejoiced. They felt honored and blessed to suffer on behalf of Christ.

I truly believe that all this is part of God's plan. I may not understand it. I may not like the timing of it, but I do know that all things work together for good to those who love God. I am open to God using me in whatever way he chooses. He has given me the gift of an amazing husband and allowed me to experience true selfless love through him, for which I am so grateful. In death, I have the gift of eternal life, a new and flawless body that is without pain and cancer. No matter what we face, there is no obstacle in the world that can keep us from God's love.

Sue Buzzeo lives with her husband Mark in Newcastle-upon-Tyne, England

CHAPTER 6

SUFFERING AND THE SOVEREIGNTY OF GOD

Sue Buzzeo's story takes us into a world of acknowledged wrong decisions and a divinely-orchestrated return to God, followed by years of serving God faithfully in the midst of life-threatening illness. What she didn't record was how all the while she continued to fulfill highly responsible positions in the business world, while also serving her community as a magistrate. One of her pastors told me every time she gave her testimony God showed up. At the end of it all, Sue staked everything on the truth of God's Word that whatever has happened in life, he works all things together for good. She determined to serve him regardless and make the most of the time he had given her.

How does God move in the midst of our decisions, good or bad, and his will? There are no contradictions in the Bible, but there are some tensions. Tensions occur in those places where two seemingly opposite sides of a situation are presented, yet both are pictured as true. For instance, think of the fact that God is totally and completely sovereign. Then think of the fact that God holds us entirely accountable for our decisions. Think of the fact that when Adam fell, we all fell. Then think of the fact that God says each of us is responsible for our own sin. These truths are resolved in the mind of God, who sees how it all works together. But our limited human intellect can only comprehend so much. The Bible addresses us in our limited ability to understand, and presents us with both sides as truth.

In the same way, the Bible tells us that the reality of the compassion, mercy and kindness of God are absolute truths to be held on to. Yet so also is the fact that in this life, we as Christians will experience suffering. My task here is not to resolve the tension, but to present it, and yet to *present it in such a way that it helps us understand how to live victoriously and with joy in the midst of it.*

One of the clearest places in the Bible to start is in Romans 8. In Romans chapters 6 through 8, we get a panoramic picture of the Christian life. We are freed from sin, yet we still fight against it (chapter 6). We are freed from the just condemnation of the law, yet we struggle to fulfill God's righteous demands on our lives (chapter 7). We are liberated into a new life by the power of the Spirit, yet we still face the reality of pain and suffering (chapter 8).

Let's zero in on the middle part of chapter 8, for there we find some foundations we can use for the rest of this book, and hopefully for the rest of our lives. First, we have a tremendous affirmation of our freedom and new life in Christ. Here's what Paul says, "For you did not receive the spirit of slavery to fall back into fear, but you have received the Spirit of adoption as sons, by whom we cry, "Abba! Father!" (Rom. 8:15).

Let's stop for a minute and unpack the full significance and power of this statement. Above everything else, God is a Father. That is part of what is expressed in the eternal interrelationship of the Trinity. He was a Father before he became a Creator. As a Father, what he desires most of all is sons and daughters, and that is why he went to the lengths he did to make that possible. It is only through the cross that anyone can enter his family. There is no other way. If it is in his nature to be a Father, it must be in our nature to be sons and daughters. That is why it is so natural for us to cry out, "Abba, Father." The word "Abba" represents the Aramaic word for "father". Aramaic was the language closely related to Hebrew which Jesus likely spoke. Originally used by small children as the equivalent of "daddy," by the time of Jesus *abba* was a more general word for father. A grown man might use it to address his dad. So while it may not be quite as familiar a term as "daddy," it was intimate enough that it was never used at all by the Jews as a form of address to God. *It expresses an intimacy and sense of relationship with God never before known in the history of humanity, in Israel or anywhere else.*

Paul did not invent the use of this word. He heard about it from those older in the faith than him, from those who had been with Jesus the night before he was crucified. For it was in Gethsemane, at his most desperate hour, that Jesus used this word both to appeal to his Father and to submit to his Father's will, "Abba, Father, all things are possible for you. Remove this cup from me. Yet not what I will, but what you will" (Mk. 14:36). When Jesus addressed God in this way, he was drawing attention to the intimacy of relationship the word expressed. This very relationship was lost in Adam, but is restored to us in Christ. It is made effective in our lives through the work of the Holy Spirit. The Holy Spirit, Paul says, assures our spirit that we are the children of God. Deep in our hearts, the Holy Spirit is at work, and the fruit of this assurance is that we can cry "Father" to God, and also that we can walk in obedience to the Father through the Spirit's power. All of this is possible only through what Jesus did for us. *To live as a Christian means to live as God's sons and daughters, and as heirs of all God's promises, and by the Spirit's power, to cry out "Father" to God in all we say and do.*

But as Paul continues, he brings even better news. We are not only God's children, we are his heirs, "The Spirit himself bears witness with our spirit that we are children of God, and if children, then heirs — heirs of God and fellow heirs with Christ" (Rom. 8:16-17a). The image, of course, is not perfect, in that God is not about to die. But Jesus did die for us, and his death has released an incredible inheritance to us. Heb. 9:15-17 explains how the result of the death of Jesus is like the contents of a will coming into effect, with us as the beneficiaries. We have eternal life, we have the gift of the Holy Spirit, we have "tasted the goodness of the word of God and the powers of the age to come" (Heb. 6:4-5).

But now comes the crunch. There are two sides to this. And both are true, though it does not seem possible. We are indeed God's heirs, but only *on one condition*, "provided we suffer with him in order that we may also be glorified with him" (Rom. 8:17b). How can this be? Our instinctive reaction is to say that suffering cannot be part of God's incredible plan for us. Does not suffering put a question mark beside whether God truly accepts or loves us? Did not Jesus himself say that even an evil father gives his children only good gifts (Lk. 11:13)? So if we are suffering, God must have rejected us. But no, says Paul, the opposite is true. We can only be heirs of God *if we suffer*. And our suffering is in fact a condition of our future glorification. When we meet him face to face, God will be looking for whether or not we have truly suffered.

Let me stop for a moment to say something important. Whatever we are going to say about suffering does not suggest that any suffering we experience adds to the saving work of Christ's suffering on the cross. *Our suffering is only part of our response of obedience to the One whose suffering alone saved us.* Jesus said, "If anyone would come after me, let him deny himself and take up his cross and follow me" (Mk. 8:34). *Jesus' death saved us only because it was preceded by a perfect life.* Two criminals suffered and died with him on Roman crosses that day, and their suffering and death saved no one.

We travel a road in this life between our conversion and our entrance into the presence of the Lord. It is a glorious road, a path of life, liberty and joy. Yet suffering is a necessary part of that road. It is built into the DNA of every Christian because it was part of the DNA of Christ.

Yet suffering is not the ultimate goal of the Christian life. It is part of the road, but not part of the destination. Paul continues, "For I consider that the sufferings of this present time are not worth comparing with the glory that is to be revealed to us" (Rom. 8:18). The entire section following (verses 19-30) explains the meaning of the tension between present suffering and future glory. In these verses, Paul is not afraid to shy away from the painful realities of this present life. Yet he urges us to focus on the hope that is to come and the certainty of its fulfillment.

He starts with the thought that the creation itself is suffering and will not be set free until we are glorified (verses 19-21). The purpose of creation was to reflect the glory of the One who created it. It cannot fulfill its destiny because of the curse God placed on the earth, "Cursed is the ground because of you" (Gen. 3:17). Ecological movements without a Christian basis and empty of the power of the Holy Spirit will either fail or fall drastically short. Why? They have no ability to change the hearts of the people who treat their environment so badly. Yet in spite of the curse, there is now hope. The creation will one day be transformed. The fact it will not be simply discarded motivates Christians to be the very best stewards of the creation as it exists now. In the same way, we are to steward our own physical bodies on account of our belief in their resurrection.

The creation groans "in the pains of childbirth" (verse 22). Christians who have the first fruits of the Spirit do the same as we await our future hope, the redemption of our bodies (verse 23). The first fruits in the Old Testament were a gift of humanity to God of the initial part of the harvest, signifying the full tithe yet to come. Here Paul reverses the idea. God is now the giver of the first fruits to us. The first fruits are the present working of the Spirit in our hearts. It is not the Spirit himself who is the first fruits. It is *his present work in us.* His future work will be the fulfillment. If the Spirit himself were the first fruits, it would diminish who he is. Why? Because it would suggest that in the future life we would have something *more or better than* the Spirit. And here again is a tension. We have the Spirit, yet not in the fullness we will experience in the future. In the same way, we are sons and daughters, yet we await our adoption (verse 23). We have it, and yet we don't have it! All these are ways of describing the tension of two truths. In different ways, Paul is trying to answer the question of suffering. Our lives are changed, yet we still await a change. We have a real hope, but for something we do not yet see (verse 24). And so we wait with patience (verse 25).

But we do not wait alone. We wait with the help of the Spirit who lives within us. The degree to which the Spirit is involved in strengthening us is powerfully portrayed in verse 26. He intercedes for us with "groanings too deep for words." He comes down to us and travails in this birth process alongside us. This is an incredible picture of the grace of God. These groanings of the Spirit are effective, whether they are articulated in words or not. Why? Because God himself, who searches our hearts, knows the mind of the Spirit (verse 27). God is listening to our cry, because he is listening to the cry of his own Spirit. As the Spirit groans within us, God hears our cry and comforts us. We have supernatural life within us, which strengthens us in the battle.

This leads us right into verse 28, one of the most loved and quoted verses in the Bible. The reason for its popularity is that it speaks right into the middle of the tension between our joy and our suffering. There are several things that are really significant in this verse. For a start, the phrase "For those who love God" is placed at the beginning of the Greek sentence and is a little out of order. Why? To give it greater emphasis! *It is a promise to believers only.* It is for those who love God and those alone that "all things work together for good." Those who love God will suffer, but their suffering has a purpose in God's plan. Why do I say this? Because of the second significant thing in this verse: the "all things" are the hard things. The "all things" are the things he has been talking about throughout this passage, the "sufferings of this present time" (verse 18). Verses 19-30 explain the relationship between these sufferings and the glory to come. Believers need no assurance that the good things of life are working for good. *What they need to know is that God is in charge of the bad things.* Anyone can make pleasant things work for good, but only God can do it with the hard things.

And now to the third significant point in verse 28, the meaning of the phrase "for good." We all want things to turn out for good. But who is allowed to define the good? I know what I think is good, and most of that is what is convenient, pleasurable, profitable and positive, the things that bring me joy and happiness. But in truth only God can define the good. *The good represents his will for me.* It may not represent my comfort or pleasure in the short term, but it is what will ultimately give me joy, as God works out his plan in my life. How important it is for us to allow God to define the good! If we define it, we will quickly find that God is not responding to our prayers by producing the happiness that we want (the good as we see it). But for the obedient believer, even the difficult things (such as the tribulations of verse 35) draw us closer to God. In the garden, our attempt to eat the tree of the knowledge of good and evil led us down a destructive path where we tried to seize the right to define what is good and what is not. God paid the ultimate price in the death of his Son to reverse the curse brought about by our sin. Part of that reversal is giving us the ability to allow him once again to define what is good for us. Because of the sin that still affects this world, the quest for the good will not come without price. But the message of this verse assures us it is a price worth paying.

And now to the last point of significance in the verse. We are called "according to his purpose." This means God has a destiny for each one of us. Our true fulfillment in this life will only come in pursuing it. Paul began this verse with the thought of us loving God, and concludes it with the thought of God calling us. *The fact that he calls us makes everything else we do in response possible.* John expresses the same thing a bit differently, "We love because he first loved us" (1 Jn. 4:19). The certainty of our hope as we travel along a road which includes suffering rests not on the fact that we love God, but on the fact that God has loved, called and chosen us.

The last two verses we are highlighting here, verses 29-30, use a chain of five verbs to describe God's gracious choosing of his people. This unbreakable chain portrays the hand of a sovereign, loving and merciful God on our lives. It cannot be broken or negated by outward negative circumstances. The first statement is this, "those whom he foreknew…" God speaks of knowing Abraham (Gen. 18:19), knowing Jeremiah (Jer. 1:5) and knowing Israel (Am. 3:2). Included in the Hebrew concept of *God's knowing a person is God's knowing his purpose for the person.* This knowing occurs before creation, in the realm of God's eternal existence. Paul emphasizes this by speaking here of God's "*fore*knowing." Peter also says we are chosen "according to the foreknowledge of God the Father" (1 Pet. 1:2).

Now comes the second link in the chain, "… he also predestined to be conformed to the image of his Son." The second verb ("predestined") describes God's gracious decision, taken before the world's foundation, concerning the purpose for which he created us. We are to become like Christ. All the lofty and sometimes incomprehensible arguments about predestination can be boiled down to this: *God cannot know a person and the purpose for which that person was created without also having a plan to implement what is contained in his knowledge.* God wants to restore us to his image, the image in which we were created (Gen. 1:27), but lost when Adam sinned. Here is an amazing truth, which should electrify us. Before even we fell, God had put in place his plan of restoration. *Before a disaster happens in your life, God has a plan to bring good out of it.* No wonder Paul can say that all things work together for good in the lives of believers!

The third link is this, "Those whom he predestined he also called." This word brings us out of eternity, and into the history of our encounter with Christ. God's calling and our conversion are two sides of the same coin. Here is that tension again. I cannot resolve it, but I can suggest it is safe to put greater emphasis on God's sovereignty than on our free will. Why? Because in the end, we want a sovereign God ruling our lives and our world. A limited God is no God at all. And our free will can only come from one place — God himself. We can say we have free will, yet the deeper truth is God has more free will than we do.

Finally, the fourth and fifth links, "Those whom he called, he also justified, and those whom he justified he also glorified." Being justified we can understand, but how can Paul say we have already been glorified? Paul uses the past tense here partly because, from God's perspective, our glorification has already been set in motion. Its fulfillment is so certain it can be spoken of as an accomplished fact. The statement back in verse 18 that the glory of God is to be revealed in us suggests that the glory is already here but not fully manifest. If you are a Christian, no matter how bleak the outward circumstances may be, never forget that the glory of God resides in you!

And so, with the promise of the glory of God in us, Paul comes back in verse 29 to where he began in verse 17. We are heirs of God, if we share in Christ's sufferings, the ultimate goal being that we might share also in his glory. The path to glory is the way of the cross. Yet even in our trials and sufferings, God has a glory stored up for us. The resurrection came after the cross. Victory is certain. But what we need is an honest understanding of the battle we face. Following Christ does not exempt us from suffering. It may in fact involve us in deeper suffering than if we lived a selfish life based on our own comfort, defining our own good.

But if we can keep our eyes on him, everything else will fall into place. What we need is the gift of confidence in the sovereign ability of God to use all the circumstances of our lives, the good, the bad and the ugly, to accomplish his eternal and glorious purposes.

REFLECTIONS FOR DISCUSSION:

After reading this chapter, what does the Biblical portrayal of God as *Abba* mean to you? How have you experienced this aspect of God's character in your personal walk with him? Has this been taught and experienced sufficiently in church? How can we represent this dimension of the character of God to others?

Suffering is part of the journey, not part of the destination. How can this help us in our walk with God? Have you experienced the "groanings of the Spirit" in your communion with the Lord?

What does it mean practically for us to allow God to define the good he promises to work all things for? Have you seen God work in your life to redefine what you thought was good and reset your understanding of what was happening in your life?

CHAPTER 7

THE WAY OF THE CROSS

The sixteenth chapter of Matthew contains a story that starts with Jesus asking the question of his disciples, "Who do people say that the Son of Man is?" (verse 13). He knows what they are thinking, but he also knows their thinking needs to be adjusted if they are to be of any use to God at all. Peter has a revelation about Jesus. He is greater than John the Baptist or Elijah, or any of the other prophets of old. He is the Christ, the Messiah, the One all Israel for centuries had been hoping for (verse 16). For the Jewish people of the first century, the Messiah would come as the Son of David. His mission would be to restore the kingdom to the greatness of David's day. He would do this by driving out the Roman invaders and restoring Israel as a great and independent nation. There is no doubt Peter and the other disciples saw Jesus this way, which is why they begged him for seats of power at his right and left. But Peter has grasped a critical part of the truth. He understands that Jesus is completely different from all those who have gone before, and that he has been sent by God to do something completely unparalleled in history.

And so Jesus responds by saying that Peter is the rock on which he will build his church (verse 18). This has got nothing to do with Peter being the first Pope! Jesus doesn't say anything about who is going to follow Peter as leader, or if indeed anyone at all will follow him. Peter's name means "rock" in Greek, and Jesus is using this play on words to say in perfectly clear language that Peter is a rock, a foundation stone, and on this rock he will build his church. Peter has a unique historical role as the first primary leader Jesus chose. Jesus tells Peter he will build his church on this human foundation. And against it, the gates of hell will not prevail, for Jesus is about to destroy the power of death.

And to Peter, as first leader, would be given the keys of this Messianic kingdom. The primary reference of the keys is the effect of the presentation of the Gospel as it goes forth across the world. The preaching of the Word unlocks the gates of salvation for those God has chosen, as they respond to it in faith. God appoints leaders, hundreds of thousands of them, who have followed in Peter's footsteps, who are given the task of administering God's household not as owners, but as stewards. They cannot control who gets in. Only the owner can do that. But they do determine how well the household runs. The literal meaning of verse 19 is that what we bind shall already have been bound, and what we loose shall already have been loosed. Leaders have no authority to make up their own rules for the household. All they can do is administer the rules that have already been put in place.

But next, Jesus draws an unexpected application. It is necessary that he go to Jerusalem, there to suffer and to die (verse 21). But for Peter, this is unthinkable. He is still basking in the glow of the authority he has been given. Jesus is going to come, drive out the Romans, and Peter is to be installed as his right hand man. No, he must have thought. This is wrong, it cannot be. So he takes Jesus aside, and he does something quite shocking: he rebukes him. The goal Jesus has set cannot be the purpose of God. It's not a goal at all, it's a disaster in the making. Peter loses sight, as we so often do, that God's ways are not our ways. The very thing we are pursuing is anathema to God, and the thing we least want is the very thing God is after.

Jesus understands in Peter's words a temptation similar to what he had faced in the wilderness, to submit to Satan, to turn aside from the way to which God had called him, to take the easy, painless route to power. Satan reappears in Peter's thinking (verse 23). This thinking must be driven out of Peter, because as long as it has a foothold, the rock that Peter represents, the rock that is critical for the establishment of the church on earth, will crumble at the first test.

And so in verse 24, Jesus begins to teach us *how to think as God thinks*. To follow him is to take up the cross. To deny oneself, to take up the cross, are Greek aorist tenses, expressing a decisive, one-off action. But then he gives a third command, "Follow me." This command is in the present tense, meaning an ongoing, continuous action. To follow Jesus is a life-long application of the first two decisions. To take up the cross is not a call to self-denial, to doing without chocolate in Lent, to give a few dollars to the church, to lend a helping hand to people when it suits. No, it is far more than a call to self-denial. *It is a call to die.* The cross was not an inconvenience, it was an instrument of death.

What does this death mean for us? It might mean actual death, but for most of us it is death to the things of this world. Jesus defines this kind of death as losing our life in order to find it (verse 25). When Jesus speaks of gaining the whole world but forfeiting one's soul (verse 26), he is referring to that moment when Satan tempted him by offering him authority over the world (Mt. 4:8-10). The things this world has to offer corrupt us and take us out of the purposes of God and the destiny he has for us. Only when material things mean nothing, only when worldly success means nothing, only when the recognition and honor of people means nothing, can we possibly be entrusted with any of those things without them destroying our life in God.

There is pain in following the way of the cross. There's all kinds of it. There's rejection, there's giving without receiving, there's much sacrificed and often little repaid. Israel's Messiah, the one they thought would drive the oppressors out, died on a Roman cross, his only possessions auctioned off by the soldiers.

Yet from that cross, he both controlled and changed the course of history. Why is the pain worth it? Because the man who died on that cross is now ruling the universe from the right hand of God (Eph. 1:20). And he is coming back "with his angels in the glory of his Father, and then he will repay each person according to what he has done" (Mt. 16:27). He died as a criminal and an outcast. But he will return as King, as Lord and as Judge. And he will repay. Sometimes we think of this simply in terms of judgment. But he also comes to repay in blessing. God is no man's debtor. What we reap is what we have sown (Gal. 6:7). It is an unbreakable law written into the heart of the universe as God created it.

There are many reasons we could give for following Jesus. The life he calls us to is not all suffering or pain. Even now we begin to reap what we have sown, even now he begins to repay. But what he is dealing with in his encounter with Peter is a lie that threatened to invade and corrupt the very foundation of his church. And this is a critical problem, because his church is the only instrument through which the power of his kingdom comes. When our thinking is that Jesus came into this world to make things easier for us, to meet our needs, to make us feel better, to take away all pain, this is the kind of thinking that makes Jesus a mere means to a happier life, not the Lord of the universe and King of creation. When this thinking creeps into our minds, it will corrupt and ruin us for any useful purpose in the mission to which God has called us. We will judge everything, the church, other Christians, even God himself, by what he or they should do for us.

Jesus calls us to the same thinking he called Peter to that day: be prepared to die. When that is the framework, the foundation, the cornerstone of our understanding of what it means to follow him, then the rest, including his blessings, including his provision, his healing, and his peace, can come into place without corrupting us.

Satan still comes with his deceptive call. We need to stand against it. You can't negotiate, compromise or bargain with the devil. You have to oppose him. Even as a Christian, you have a choice: you can be part of God's foundation, or you can be an obstacle in God's way. None of us really knows at the outset what it truly means to take up the cross and follow Christ. As we follow, it becomes clearer. If we've truly made the commitment, nothing will turn us aside. Whatever price God calls us to pay, the reward, both now and in eternity, is forever and always worth it.

REFLECTIONS FOR DISCUSSION:

Following Jesus is a life-long application of our initial decision to deny ourselves and take up the cross. How has this worked in your life? Has it enabled you to process suffering redemptively?

Is it possible, in this life, to begin to learn to think as God thinks and how do we do it? How often have you missed or misunderstood God because of a failure to think as God thinks? Reflect on an occasion when that happened.

CHAPTER 8

GOD DIDN'T PROMISE ME A SON

Malyn Sneed

It was a morning just like all the rest. Actually it was pretty peaceful. The girls were off to school and Brian was working from home. I was doing household chores and cleaning out closets in the children's rooms. Meanwhile our newly adopted son, Camden David, was fast asleep in his crib. I was working in the room right beside his. I had checked on him often as he was sleeping late this particular morning, but it definitely wasn't the first time he had done so. The last time, I went in with plans to wake him up, and our lives changed forever.

He wasn't breathing. I screamed for my husband. Thank God he was home that day. Brian ran in, scooped him up, and immediately started to perform CPR as I called 911. I was frantic. I could barely talk to the 911 dispatcher, but she was so gracious and walked us through each step. His lungs filled up with air one time and he opened his eyes. The words from my husband in these moments are forever engrained in my memory: *"God please don't take my son!"* It was from the depths that he cried out. The ambulance seemed to arrive in just one minute. They said there were some good signs. I had hope.

On the way to the hospital, Brian and I prayed with every ounce of faith in our being. We were pleading aloud with the Father and claiming a miracle. I vowed to give God all the glory for the miracle that would take place. And there really wasn't a doubt in my mind that it would happen.

When we arrived at the emergency room, nobody could tell us anything. The ambulance had just arrived a few moments before and there was no news. I just wanted to know if he was breathing. I saw police officers enter and for the first time, my mind went to the worst place. I've seen enough criminal shows to know this didn't seem good. Brian tried to comfort me. He explained officers could be there for other reasons. We continued to pray.

We were moved to a smaller, private room while we waited for the doctor. The doctor and nurse walked in and said he didn't make it. It's all a little hazy after this. It seemed like things were moving in slow motion. I remember Brian throwing his phone down. I remember falling to my knees and all I could cry was, "NO." I remember seeing my dad through the privacy glass at the door to this little room, and shaking my head no to let him know. I was in disbelief and shock. I couldn't breathe. I felt like someone had punched me in the gut.

I instantly blamed myself. I should have done something different. I should have slept with him. I shouldn't have let him sleep in. And I will never forget the nurse that came and held me and said, "No, don't do this. You're a believer, and if you believe, then you know that our days are numbered. There was nothing you could do. It was his time." I didn't know her at all, but looking back I am so grateful for the wisdom in her words.

At that moment though all I could feel was the pain. Family and friends started to pour into the little room, along with counsellors. Where was I? How did I get here? It honestly seemed like a nightmare or a really awful movie, but not my life. In fact, I didn't feel any life, just the sting of death. We got escorted back to see our little boy one more time. His jammies were cut. He was getting cold. I kissed his face and told him I loved him more than he could ever know, and I was so thankful God chose me to be his mommy. And I told him I couldn't wait to see him again. Brian said, "Where's my boy at?" He used to say that to him all the time and Camden would pop up and say, "Here I am!" Brian told him how he wanted to take him fishing. There were so many memories we had looked forward to creating with him. The officer that escorted us back to the exam room stood there trying to remain professional, but as we were exiting the room I saw the tears in his eyes.

We walked out of the emergency room that day without our son. It was winter. There was snow on the ground, and the bitter cold wind slapped me in the face as we crossed through those doors. This was reality.

I began to think about how we would break this news to our girls. They had a snow day with their baby brother the day before this where they had all climbed up and down their new bunk bed. They went to school every other day and expected to come home and see him. Would they hate me? Would they think there was something else I should have done? Would they be afraid to sleep? I'm their mom. I should have been able to protect every single one of them. I wanted to have been able to protect him, and now I wanted to find a way to protect my girls' hearts. I knew there was no way. No matter what we said or did, they were going to feel something nobody should ever have to feel, and especially at their age. It wasn't fair. When we shared the news with them, my heart shattered again. I had already experienced the worst of the worst that day, and now here I was feeling it all over again, along with such a sense of helplessness.

Over the next few days, our house was full of family and the most amazing friends you could imagine. Our incredible church family were there around the clock caring for us, cooking for us, doing laundry, and helping with the kids. Friends very dear to our hearts traveled from the north and south to be with us in our darkest days. Everyone rallied around us in prayer and even financial support. This was different. We're usually on the giving end, and I much prefer that. The outpouring of love we were shown still overwhelms me.

When visitors left and friends returned to work, it was quiet in the house. I usually enjoy the quiet, but not this time. I wasn't hungry. I couldn't sleep. I just felt sick. Brian did a lot of working from home and making sure friends could be over for me if he couldn't. Everything felt surreal. As our nine year old daughter Kaelyn put it, "It just seems like he went on a little trip and he will be back, but when I realize he won't be back, I just can't imagine that." We were facing the unimaginable.

We went from the greatest day of our lives to the worst in less than a month. We had been on a foster journey with Camden since April of 2014. And all of the ups and downs and fears had only just subsided when we were finally able to adopt him on December 23, 2015. Our girls said he was the best Christmas present ever. He was finally a Sneed.

"Gotcha Forever" were the words on his new adoption sign. But January 13, 2016 was a game changer I never saw coming. I never foresaw choosing an outfit for my two year old son to be buried in, or receiving his death certificate before I even received his birth certificate. It honestly just felt cruel. I battled it out with God. I was confused, hurt, angry and heart broken. For the first time in my life, I felt as though he had left me, and I let him know all about it. I was actually praying for a resurrection miracle all the way up until we buried Camden. I was now at the point where I questioned everything I had believed in my whole life. Of course I still believed in God. I just wondered where he was on that day, and of course I wondered why this had to happen. I wondered if God even knew the pain of losing my only son, and then I was quickly reminded of how he gave up his only son and why he did it.

Which leads me to Easter. When I look at Christ's journey to the cross, it seems to parallel the unimaginable journey I'm on in many ways. Palm Sunday was a day filled with excitement, much like December 23 was for us, the day Camden had his own triumphal entry into our family.

But things for Jesus changed so quickly, and for us too. I wanted more of the beautiful moments, more time, and I certainly didn't want this. *This* had never crossed my mind. I never considered anything other than watching my only son grow into a God-fearing young man, protecting his sisters, playing ball with his daddy, and loving his mama the way boys do. After all, I waited for this little boy. Good things come to those who wait, right? It was a roller coaster of trials, patience, and emotions to get to that perfect "gotcha" day!

I imagine that for Mary, Jesus' mother, Friday came too soon, and there probably wasn't much good she saw in it. My Good Friday happened to be a Wednesday, the day death was so real and in my face. The day I walked out of that hospital without my son. Mary had to go home without her son too. Yet in spite of all the things stripped from both of us on those dreadful days, the promise of Jesus couldn't be taken away. The promise of hope and new life was something he sealed the deal on when he rose from the grave that Sunday.

Around Easter we always hear the phrase, "It's Friday, but Sunday is coming!" But what about Saturday, the day in between the tragedy and the promise? It was a day filled with hurt, sadness, confusion, maybe some doubt, mourning, lots of waiting, and extreme faith testing. That doesn't sound like much fun, so who wants to talk about it? I do. Saturday is important, because Saturday is the day you find out what you're made of, what you believe in, and how deeply rooted you are or not. Saturday is the day between the tragedy and the promise. *Your response on Saturday sets the course for your life.* It determines where you're going with Jesus on this path that's not your own. My hope is rooted in eternity, not Saturday.

As the days went on, Brian and I would be up all night watching our girls sleep. How could we do otherwise? But I also kept trying to check on their emotional state. Kids are amazingly resilient, but I knew they were devastated. Our oldest, Skyler, who was sixteen at the time, set a wonderful example for the younger girls. Camden was almost like her little baby, as she always acted as "mom" when I was absent. For a very long time, she couldn't go into his room. She was the only one who understood the full impact of our words the night we broke the awful news. Yet somehow she found the most beautiful words to share at his funeral. She carried herself with such grace in the midst of deepest sorrow.

Kaelyn, who was eight, is our thinker. But she's also the most sensitive of the three girls. She served me in the most gracious way while I tried to keep everything together, and even at eight showed such care for Kalli, who at five was the youngest. I was especially worried about her as I knew she would have the hardest time communicating how she felt. She was experiencing brokenness all too soon, and that in turn broke me. She took to holding a teddy bear in place of him. Camden gave her the long sought after title of "big sister." There's nothing I could do to take the pain away, not even in all my superhero power as Mommy. I played the song "How long will I love you?" over and over while looking through pictures of Camden. When I asked if she would like to build a playlist so she didn't have to keep hearing the same song she quietly replied, "No, this one reminds me of Cam."

Life is a gift, but unless you've ever stared death in the face while that gift is being stripped away, you may not realize how precious it truly is. The number of days you hold your babies, wipe snotty noses, change stinky diapers, be the taxi driver, chef, secretary, be the biggest cheerleader, referee, and coach — those days are a high privilege. They are days to celebrate. Pay attention moms. You're building something here that is far more significant than the routine tasks that burn you out. Look beyond it. Life at any stage is worth celebrating, and don't miss any part of it.

In every celebration, there's something to miss. When your baby becomes a toddler it's exciting to watch them grow, but you miss the tender baby scent and snuggles. When your baby turns sixteen and you watch them pull out of the driveway, you're proud, nervous, and scared all at the same time, but you miss having them home. Celebrations and memories go hand in hand. And because there was such a huge hole in our family where Camden once was, celebrations became so much different. The span of emotions was just indescribable. I hope I'm not being a downer. I just don't want to slap a happy face on something that isn't always happy. It's incredibly hard to truly celebrate much of anything without missing him terribly. We do cling to a living hope, but it still hurts. That's just truth.

As I sat beside Kalli a few weeks later, I felt I had nothing to offer her except my love. I wondered if this was how God was feeling about me. I wondered if it hurt him to look at me as he stood there with his arms wide open.

On January 27, two weeks after Camden went to heaven, I documented a Wednesday with my little girls.

My journal read:

"Spent the day with Kaelyn. She was brave, just as she's been this whole time. We had such a great time together. We spent over two hours in Target and saw a few things Cam would love there which she pointed out — paw patrol boots, cute little plaid shirts, and so on. I asked her how she was doing. We talked about how we missed him and I asked if I could do anything to help her. She said no, paused, and then said, 'Unless you could bring him back for me.' As we were driving home from our fun day suddenly it all came back again. Church was hard tonight, especially prayer service. Hearing people pray, hearing my dad pray over people saying how God wasn't a God who might help but who will help. And all I could feel was 'but he DIDN'T.' Why?? Why didn't he? Brian and I had prayed with every ounce of faith we have and told God we would give him all the glory for breathing life into Camden's lungs. I continued to pray he would raise him up until the very time we buried him. But it didn't happen. And now I'm listening to other people's prayers that honestly seem so insignificant right now. I trusted God with my whole life, my only son, who was just given to me. And it felt like he left me. The worship team started to sing, 'You are perfect in all of your ways.' I couldn't bring myself to utter those words. This is so far from perfect, God. I stayed for service, but I got the girls and bolted as fast as I could afterward. It was a hard night for them too. I think it was the first time we realized everyone else's life keeps moving and ours is on the most painful pause. Kaelyn choked up on the way home. She feels like he went with someone on a trip and he will be back, but he won't. Kalli cried and told me at school they had to pick their favorite season and she said winter. I was shocked because the kids love summer time with the pool. She said this: 'I want it to stay winter so we don't have to put a stone on Camden's grave.' I guess somehow in her mind the headstone seals the deal for her. I love how both of our little girls have clung to the truth that Camden is with Jesus in the perfect place. They don't ask for reasons and they don't even ask many 'whys.' Childlike faith. Trusting in the dark, when you can't see a thing, and all you can feel is pain."

I apologize if the journal entry is a bit too raw, but it's the place I was in. I do still believe every detail is important to God and every prayer is significant. I also do realize God never left me. He's been walking it out with me just as he promised. It was just a little harder to see it on that day. People have told me I'm incredibly strong. The truth is I'm not. Some days I'm ready to go to battle, and some days I would rather not get out of my bed. But God gives grace for each new day, in every situation, sometimes minute by minute. I still don't understand it, but I don't try to figure it out. I know that if there were no pain, we wouldn't need a Savior. If there were no brokenness, we wouldn't need a Redeemer. And if there were no memories, there wouldn't be celebrations. I'm thankful for the memories that will one day turn into an amazing celebration.

In my darkest times when I felt the most alone, I also felt closest to God. It's hard to describe that feeling, but there was a longing in my heart for heaven I had never experienced before. I've never dreamed so much of heaven. I want to see it, touch it, feel it, and in brief moments I do feel it. It just confirms that God's promises are real and true.

I thought a lot about God's promises during this time, when everything around me was crumbling. And I thought about this phrase: *God didn't promise me a son.* Those were the words I typed on January 10, three days before my son went to heaven. It was early Sunday morning, and my husband was asking me for examples of a time I had prayed in faith, not knowing the outcome, and received something so much greater than I could have ever dreamed of. This gift of Camden showed me God knows and fulfills desires and promises we don't even know about yet. Kind of like when you have a big surprise for your own kids.

Camden David was my big surprise. We went into fostering him not knowing what the outcome would be. We didn't have to spend months in prayer about loving this little boy because Jesus had already commanded us to do so. We had read it in the Bible, "Religion that is pure and undefiled before God, the Father, is this: to visit orphans and widows in their affliction " (Jas. 1:27). Adding a baby in the mix as we prepared to plant a church in Kalamazoo was crazy, but we decided we were going to love this kid like nobody's business. We didn't know what the outcome would be when we committed to love him. We didn't know if we would be able to adopt him, or if he would end up with his biological family. However, it wasn't up to me. I couldn't focus on the outcome. I just needed to trust.

That Sunday morning, Brian preached on prayer. He said it's not important how you pray, but that you pray. He said it's important not to predetermine the outcome of prayer. And he said that the most crucial aspect of prayer is making yourself available for God. He said often God's will for us involves situations we aren't comfortable with. He said we become fearful as we try to imagine how we can ensure positive outcomes. But we just have to trust God. If we are obedient, Jesus will look after the rest.

Looking back, I think about all we would have missed with our precious boy if we had needed to know the outcome in order to start the journey. Fear of the unknown holds so many back from what could be their greatest adventures. And he was our greatest adventure and our biggest joy.

God didn't promise me a son. I don't know exactly why God gave me those words that Sunday. But the following Wednesday, when my world fell apart, in my desperate crying out, my mind instantly went back to them. And if I'm honest, it made me angrier than anything on that day when I felt like I couldn't find Jesus. But even in the most gut wrenching pain, when I went back to those words I couldn't deny he had been there the whole time. The words are true. I didn't foster him because I had a promise of a son. I actually had no idea if we would get to adopt him. I had dreams and hopes too, but I had surrendered them to God. I had no idea what that surrendering would cost me. We say we trust God with our kids and we dedicate them to him, but you really rethink that vow when something like this happens.

As the days went on I reread those words many times. Was God trying to prepare me? He knows all. He had Camden's days numbered (Ps. 139:16). Did he want me to know he wasn't breaking any promise to me and he hated to see my heart breaking like this? I like to think so. He's got my best interest at heart, even when it hurts.

Our family took a vote after Camden went to heaven. The question was this: Even if we knew he would go to heaven so soon, would we do it all over again? Every sweet little voice said, "Yes!" The joy he brought to each and every one of us was worth the darkest pain we were all enduring.

Don't try to have it all figured out before you jump all in with God. If you do, you'll miss some of the greatest things he has for you. The greater the risk, the greater the reward. And if he's in it, the outcome will always bring him glory. And isn't that our main mission anyway?

For a long time after, people would say to me: "How do you keep doing things with a smile? How do you get out of bed every morning? How do you take care of your kids?" The only answer I had to their questions was this: *I need Jesus more than I need the answers.* That's the reason I worship through the questions and the heartbreak. Don't think there aren't still questions and awful days. Sometimes you can't imagine how bad it is. *But the other thing you can't imagine is the abundance of God's grace and strength in your life to keep going.* He tailors things just for us, for whatever season of life we're going through. He loves us that much.

Some question how we can still believe God is good. There have been many days that didn't *feel* good, but my circumstances don't dictate the goodness of my God. "Oh, taste and see that the Lord is good!" (Ps. 34:8). I can still believe that my God is good because I know him. I spend time with him. His presence overwhelms me, and his goodness is an unbreakable promise.

God didn't promise me a son. But he did promise me his Son. And that, even in the pain, is enough.

Malyn Sneed lives with her husband Brian and three daughters in Three Rivers, Michigan.

CHAPTER 9

WHEN JESUS DOESN'T SHOW UP

As a grieving mother facing inexplicable tragedy, Malyn Sneed might well have felt that Jesus hadn't shown up for her. It was a sentiment shared by two sisters who were very close to Jesus.

Mary and Martha, along with their brother Lazarus, lived at Bethany, which was about two miles from Jerusalem. That they were close friends of Jesus is clear from the sisters' message, "He whom you love is ill" (Jn. 11:3). Jesus had created such a firestorm in Jerusalem that he had barely escaped stoning (Jn. 10:31). For him to come to Bethany, on the very doorstep of Jerusalem, would mean severe danger. Yet what were the sisters to do? Their brother was dying, and Jesus was their only hope.

We may not see how God is going to be able to help us, but that is his problem. Our responsibility is to let him know our need. How often do we rationalize away the fact that God can help, and so give up before we start? The sisters were desperate. It was an impossible predicament, but they did the right thing. They asked Jesus to come, and left the rest with him.

On receiving the message, Jesus made the statement that Lazarus' illness would not end in death, but that God would be glorified through it. God has a plan and intention in everything. His plan is not tailor-made to ensure we never experience trial or distress, and this story is an illustration of that. God is not the author of evil. Trouble entered the world because of one thing only, our sin. That opened the door to the source of all evil, the devil. But God takes up the web of our disaster and weaves it into something which instead brings our deliverance. He uses the materials at hand — sickness, blindness, poverty, injustice — but turns them to gold. So here God starts not with Lazarus' healing, but with his death. Yet he is going to use that tragedy to fashion a greater triumph. How? That we will find out as the story progresses. But be warned, it may not be exactly what you expect.

Even in the most desperate of circumstances, God is working his purposes out. It is not that he has abandoned you, or is punishing you by allowing you to go through difficulties. What is happening is that he is entering into a world of hurt, suffering and pain caused by human sin. The results of this sin affect us all in various ways, even when in some circumstances (like the man born blind in John 9, or Lazarus with his incurable illness) we are apparently innocent victims. Good people and evil people alike come under the curse of physical decay and death, of relationship breakdown and all forms of human pain, for we have all sinned. Yet for the righteous, God is at work in the midst of the pain, and even death becomes the doorway to eternal life.

"Now Jesus loved Martha and her sister and Lazarus" (Jn. 11:5). Yet instead of rushing to Lazarus' help, Jesus did nothing for two long days. Time was of the essence — but not for Jesus. Without doubt, Jesus loved this family. The only conclusion we can come to is that it was *because* he loved them that he did not respond. Why? He knew God had a greater plan that no one else but him could see. Yet Jesus' response must have been a shock to his disciples.

What was in his mind? Jesus intended in the first place that God should be glorified through the raising of Lazarus from death. He waited two days before receiving a revelation that Lazarus had died. Only when he knew Lazarus had died did he set off. The 90 mile journey from the northeastern trans-Jordan region took four days, the precise period of time Lazarus had been dead when Jesus arrived. But even so, why did he wait, when he could have shortened the season of grief by raising Lazarus two days earlier than he did? The reason lies in the popular Jewish belief that the soul hovered over the deceased body for three days, intending to re-enter, but that when it was clear decomposition had set in, the soul departed permanently. A "premature" resurrection could have been interpreted by the Jews as a mere resuscitation rather than as life from the dead, and God would not have been glorified, nor would the faith of the disciples or of Mary and Martha have been increased.

And this tells us something very important. *The significance of the waiting is to show that Jesus was never moved by any human pressure or circumstance, but only by the Father's will.* Human suffering does not leave God indifferent. But neither does it force his hand. A dying brother was all that Mary and Martha could see. Yet their predicament did not cause God to act to resolve it. Jesus did not show up, but there was a reason for it invisible to the suffering family members. And sometimes we find ourselves in the same situation.

God's will is not dictated by our need. Look at the events in Cana of Galilee. There was no wine (Jn. 2:34), but Jesus did not appear concerned. Even though the need was immediate, he did not respond. Yet later on, he did. Look at what happened before the Feast of Tabernacles. Jesus' brothers urged him to go up to Jerusalem (Jn. 7:3). Surely if he wanted to be known, he should be there. He refused, because it was not the time the Father had appointed (verse 6). Yet later on, he went. And here we see the same pattern. In all three cases, someone close to Jesus — his mother, his brothers, Mary and Martha — asked him to do something which was very important to them. His refusal to respond immediately shows he was never moved by human pressure, but only acted according to the Father's will and in the Father's timing.

All we see, especially in times of crisis or suffering, is our need. But what God does is determined by the strategy he has birthed in his eternal counsel. There is always human suffering. And if that suffering is yours, and you are asking God to help you, never doubt that he will come through for you. But remember he will answer out of his loving and merciful plan for you. That plan is always for your best, even when it does not seem so to you.

That higher plan of God is now revealed. After leaving the plain of the Jordan that day, Jesus never returned. He went to Bethany and on to his death. Everyone else in the story — the sisters and the disciples — were consumed with the sickness and death of Lazarus. But Jesus had his eyes on something else. He knew that the resurrection of Lazarus would precipitate his own death, and thus his resurrection. How do we know this? Because it's made clear at the end of the story. It was as a *direct result of the resurrection of Lazarus* that the Jews determined not just to arrest Jesus, as they had previously planned, but to put him to death. In the pandemonium which ensued from Lazarus being raised from the dead, multitudes were flocking to Jesus. The rulers, realizing the situation was spiraling out of their control, gathered the council together (verse 47), where Caiaphas made the statement that one man must die for the people (verse 50). And "so from that day," John records, "they made plans to put him to death" (verse 53).

When you go to a planetarium, you can see the nearer constellations. They look so massive you think you're seeing everything there is. Then the cameras draw back the perspective so that suddenly what you saw previously as dominating the whole canvas is now only a small part of the enormously bigger universe. That's the difference between seeing with our eyes and seeing with the eyes of God. Jesus refused to live within the limiting perspective of the sisters or his mother or his brothers or his disciples. *He lived within the limitless perspective of his Father.* At the beginning of the story, Jesus made the statement that the illness of Lazarus would lead to the glorification of the Son of man. The story wasn't leading to Lazarus' resurrection (though that happened). It was leading to the death and resurrection of Jesus Christ, the arrival of the kingdom of God, and his victory over the work of the enemy. Yet only Jesus knew that. And that reveals another reason why Jesus waited. Not only because he wanted to make sure there was no doubt about the fact Lazarus was raised from the dead, but also because he had to be in Jerusalem to die at Passover, and not before. And thus to fulfill centuries of prophetic promises concerning his coming.

When confronted by crisis or suffering, we naturally see things from our own perspective. That perspective is determined by self-protection. Understandably, we want God to work things out in our lives so that we face the minimum of suffering, waiting, testing or discomfort, and have all our needs met as fully and as quickly as possible. But as in the days of Lazarus, God is working out the agenda of his kingdom. His agenda may not be to meet us in our need, or to make things easier or better. Is this because he does not love us? No, he loves us as much as Jesus loved Lazarus and his sisters. But his love for us may lead him to be more concerned about the depth of character he is building in us than what is happening to us. He may be more interested in how he is using these hard circumstances to prepare us for what he has called us to be and to do. He is often more interested in how we respond to testing than in removing the testing, because only through the testing can he produce the result — a faith purer than gold (1 Pet. 1:7). How often have you looked back on tough times and thanked God for how much you grew through them? Is it not true that most of our spiritual growth comes in the hard times rather than the easier times? Those are the times we become most dependent on him alone, because nothing else works.

But God did have a purpose for Lazarus. In verses 14-15, Jesus makes an apparently senseless and heartless declaration, "Lazarus has died, and for your sake I am glad that I was not there, so that you may believe." In a way not discernible to the human eye, God is working through difficult and even tragic events to further his deeper purposes. Why would Jesus say he was glad that anyone, let alone his dear friend Lazarus, had died? Because he had access to information that the others did not possess. He knew that Lazarus would be raised from the dead. He knew it would have an effect on the disciples' faith. The tense of the Greek verb refers to a *beginning* of believing, "so that you may *begin* to believe." They already were believers. The meaning must therefore be that their faith was about to be raised to a whole new level, "so that you are beginning to believe in a way you have never believed before." God uses impossible situations to increase our faith. Faith rarely grows in the easy times, but only when we face challenges and see God overcome them. Sometimes we have to go through a death experience to reach the place God wants us to be. In Lazarus' case, that was literally so.

We do not have the same relationship with the Father Jesus had. Yet when we face difficult situations, we do have access by the Holy Spirit to God's thoughts. That is what Paul meant when he said we have the "mind of Christ" (1 Cor. 2:16). We can begin to see things the way God does — not perfectly, but in a way unbelievers cannot perceive. And even if we cannot see why something is happening, we can still know that God is at work in it. And we can still cry out to him for deliverance, in the knowledge that he is more committed to our best interests than we are ourselves.

The story contains an interesting statement by Thomas, "Let us also go, that we may die with him" (verse 16). This has been misunderstood as some kind of sentimental or emotional reaction on Thomas' part to the death of a friend. But such is not the case. Thomas knew the danger of returning to Judea. Knowing that danger and even death lay before them if they went back there, Thomas chose to be ready to die with Christ rather than to live without him. His faith may have had its ups and downs, just like ours, but this Scripture shows why Jesus chose Thomas, with all his doubts, as one of the small group of men who would change the world.

So what is the story all about? For the sisters, the story was initially about the healing of Lazarus. That was what they came to Jesus for. For the disciples — and in the end, the sisters also — the story was about Lazarus' resurrection. But neither, in truth, was the real story. Only Jesus knew what the real story was. The real story was about his coming death and resurrection, the triumph of God over sin and death, and the inauguration of God's kingdom on earth. All of it precipitated by the miracle at Bethany.

When we are going through the struggles of life, we need God's help to answer the questions that confront us. What is the real story here? What is actually going on? What is it that God is doing above and beyond what involves only us and of which our story is only a part? What is he doing above and beyond what we can see with our human understanding? To answer these questions, we need the Holy Spirit's help. And for that, we need spiritual eyes. What is superficially seen with the human eye will pass away, but what is more deeply seen with the spiritual eye is eternal (2 Cor. 4:18).

We need to live by information from heaven if we are going to understand the story as it unfolds before us on earth. This is especially true in times of suffering. Sometimes the full story will not be known before heaven, and we have to rest content with that. But so very often, we misunderstand and misinterpret what God is doing in our lives because we don't have eyes to see and ears to hear what he is doing right in front of us. If we want to work with God and not against him, if we want to enter into all he has for us, we need to see the real story. Then, with the help of his Spirit, we can work with him toward its glorious fulfillment.

REFLECTIONS FOR DISCUSSION:

How does this chapter lead you to think about times in your life when everything seemed to go wrong and the Lord didn't show up for you? Has it helped you at all as you look back? Are there times when you have looked back and discovered how God was at work all along when he seemed to be so profoundly absent at the time?

What is the story of Lazarus about? Can you see your story in the midst of it? How do we let God in to help us better understand the process of suffering? Have you ever been through what seemed a total disaster that later turned out to produce blessing?

CHAPTER 10

OVERCOMING DISILLUSIONMENT

Luke's Gospel contains a remarkable story about two people who encounter the resurrected Christ on the road to Emmaus (Lk. 24:13-35). The story is not just about the resurrection. It's about how God's promises are fulfilled in an unexpected way. And it's about all of us who look for God's promises in the wrong places. It's about those of us who *get disillusioned because we believed an illusion.* We often evaluate the suffering and hardship we experience out of a mistaken idea of what God has promised to us. Instead of suffering becoming a doorway to a new and revived hope, it can destroy us.

The story opens with these two people journeying from Jerusalem to a village called Emmaus a few miles away. One of them is named as Cleopas (verse 18). We find him also in Jn. 19:25, though with the Hebrew spelling of his name, Clopas. And Cleopas is an important person. His wife Mary was one of the four women at the cross with Mary the mother of Jesus, her sister and Mary Magdalene. The other disciple with Cleopas on the road that day is not named. It could have been a male friend, or it could even have been Cleopas' wife.

Why were they going to Emmaus? We don't know. Perhaps in their grief they were going to visit friends, or escape to some place of safety or comfort. Perhaps they just could not bear to stay in the city which had been the place of such horror only hours before.

So here they were on the road in intense conversation (verse 14). The Greek word is *homileo*, from which we get the word for preaching. Then in verse 15, the word "discussing" really means more like "debating." They were in hot and heavy discussion. They were talking about "all the events" that had just happened. They were going over and over everything again. We can imagine their conversation, questioning God, questioning themselves, questioning Jesus. Why had that happened, how had it come to that, what are we to do, where are we to go? If they were husband and wife, you can imagine the wife pouring out her feelings, the husband trying but failing to satisfy her, as emotion pours out in massive waves over them, submerging them both in utter grief.

And suddenly Jesus himself draws by them and begins to walk alongside them, yet they do not recognize him. Why? Their eyes were kept from it (verse 16). But by whom? The answer must be by God. Satan is nowhere in the picture here, and the passive form of the verb "were kept" is a Biblical way of pointing to God as the author of the action. As the story progresses, we find their eyes had been closed in other ways also. But at this point, God does not want them to see who it is who is walking with them.

The stranger has overheard something of their conversation, and he asks them what they are talking about. His question arrests them: the Greek verb in verse 17 informs us they came to a sudden halt. And Luke adds the detail that they looked sad. This is the same word Jesus used in Mt. 6:16 of the hypocrites who "disfigure their faces" so that their fasting may be seen by others. For our two travellers, their grief was so vivid it transformed their very appearance. Cleopas responds to the stranger with astonishment. Are you the *only one* (the way he says it is emphatic) who's been in Jerusalem the last few days who *doesn't* know what happened? The death of Jesus was not something that happened in secret; the whole city knew about it. That was why the Jewish leaders had to conspire with the Roman guards to spread a false story of disciples stealing the body when it became known, as it must have done to the whole city, that the tomb of Jesus was empty. Jesus' death and empty tomb were the biggest news events of the day in Jerusalem. And that, by the way, is why no one can rationally suggest it was all a made-up story. The gospels are newspaper accounts of events as they happened. And because no one could ever explain how the body had been removed from a sealed tomb with a Roman guard, and because no one could ever find the body (and all the energy and resources of the Sanhedrin and of Rome must have been deployed in that effort), that is why the people of Jerusalem, when confronted with the falling of the Holy Spirit on Pentecost, responded in the thousands to the claim of the apostles that he was risen from the dead!

But all this was not apparent at that moment to Cleopas and his companion. Responding to the stranger, they start off with guarded statements. Jesus was a man, in fact a prophet, mighty in word and deed. Then they get a bit bolder, casting responsibility on the chief priests for his death. Finally, they reveal their true hope. Jesus was the one who was going to redeem Israel. Redemption, as N.T. Wright puts it in his book *The Challenge of Jesus*, was a "code word" for the Exodus. Redemption means freedom. The Exodus was to the Jews of Jesus' day a *political event*. It was the freeing of the children of Israel from their foreign masters. The whole thinking of the Jewish people was built around the hope that God would send *another redeemer like Moses*. Isaiah prophesied the day when God would redeem his people, "Behold, I will make of you a threshing sledge... you shall thresh the mountains and crush them... you shall winnow them, and the wind will shall carry them away..." (Isa. 41:15-16). The Old Testament is full of such promises. That's what the disciples were thinking about when they asked Jesus for places at the right and left in his kingdom. They were not envisioning the new Jerusalem of Revelation 21. They were thinking of the old Jerusalem, with Jesus ruling it instead of the Romans. Cleopas says, "We had hoped" (verse 21). The Greek tense of the verb actually expresses an ongoing action, not just the thought they had at that moment. This was the hope they had been living for; it was their whole mindset or mentality. *Incredibly, it was the mindset the disciples still had after spending three years walking with the Lord.*

But before we get too hard on Cleopas or the other disciples, we have to remember they had inherited this mentality honestly. All through the Old Testament, Israel had gained its freedom, then lost it, then cried out under terrible oppression, then regained it, then lost it once more. Finally, the Babylonians destroyed the nation and carried it off into exile. And even though the Jews eventually returned, they had never for any length of time regained their freedom. One nation after another ruled them, right up until the days of Rome. And so when Zechariah prophesied that God would raise up a man from the house of the royal line of David to save Israel from her enemies (Lk. 1:69-71), what else would any devout Jew understand than that freedom from Rome was at hand through that man? Why else would the Jewish rulers have feared that the Romans would destroy the nation on account of Jesus? Why else would Herod have been worried about him? Why else would Pilate have asked him whether he claimed to be a king?

And that's why Cleopas and his companion were in such grief that day. It wasn't just that this man they loved, admired and followed had been killed. It was that *their hope had been destroyed.* Wright makes the observation that crucifixion is what happens to someone who thought he could overthrow the government and found out too late that he couldn't. The two disciples that day were living out Psalm 42, where the Psalmist wrote of his anguish in being banished from Jerusalem, as he asks God the very question Jesus quoted on the cross, "Why have you forsaken me?" And at that very, awful moment at Calvary, his accusers shouted out and thus unwittingly fulfilled the further words of the Psalm, "My adversaries taunt me, while they say to me continually, 'Where is your God?'" (Ps. 42:10).

Cleopas and the other disciple had based their lives on a hope that had been shattered. They had gone down a road that turned out to be a dead end. Now news has come of a missing body, of an angelic visitation at the tomb, and of confirmation of these reports. But whatever had happened, it did not signify much in their eyes, for "him they did not see" (verse 24). So in spite of these extraordinary reports, their faces are still disfigured in grief. The irony is that the one they did not see is *at that moment* walking and talking with them, but they *cannot see him* because of their spiritual blindness. They cannot see him because they have been looking for him in the wrong place. They have been expecting him to do the wrong things. *This proves that even when God seems completely absent, he can be most at work.* Never judge by external circumstances. Tough times are often the best times to ask God to begin to show us what he is really but often invisibly doing behind the scenes.

So far the stranger has listened. But now he intervenes, "O foolish ones, and slow of heart to believe all that the prophets have spoken!" (verse 25). The disciples and the stranger have been reading the same story, but have understood it very differently. Wright says that the Old Testament offered to the Jewish people a story in search of an ending. The ending the disciples had expected had not come to pass, but the stranger is going to provide a different understanding of the story, and a different ending. The story is not about Israel destroying her enemies and gaining political freedom. The story is not primarily about Israel at all. It's about a man God is going to send. Beginning with Moses and the prophets, the stranger explains how the story is about that man. This man is going to enter a world of violence and suffer the worst it has to offer. He is going to be beaten, bruised, tortured and killed. He is going to do what Israel had failed to do. He is going to bring in God's kingdom, but not in the way they had anticipated. Just like it was with Moses, the victory is going to come at the very moment the darkness is greatest. God often chooses to meet his people at the screaming point. The cross was not the end, it was the beginning.

And then, when they reach their destination, the stranger makes as if to carry on, but they ask him to stay. Jesus always waits for our invitation. He stands at our door and knocks, but we have to let him in. And in the breaking of bread, the re-enactment of the last supper and the forerunner to our communion, their eyes are opened and instantly he disappears. Once real faith has come, it no longer requires sight. They turn to each other. Their darkness, in the blink of an eye, is turned into light. They hasten back to Jerusalem, the place of their defeat, to rejoice in God's victory.

How often do we walk on the road to Emmaus? How often do we misunderstand what is happening around us because we forget that God always calls us to walk in the way of the cross? How often do we sink in despair because we have wrongly evaluated our suffering? How often do we become bitter or angry because we have lived in an illusion about what God has promised? How often do we take wrong turns because of our failure to understand God and his ways? How often do we forget that God is committed to our sanctification more than our happiness, but that true joy is found in submitting to his purposes? How often because of disappointments in life do we fail to realize that Jesus is walking beside us in the midst of them because *due to our blindness we cannot see him?*

Yet also how often do we stagger away from the places of our defeat only to find Jesus along the road giving us the strength to go back and find victory in the place of our previous failure? How often above all do we forget that Jesus was not a helpless victim. No! The truth is that even as he hung on a Roman cross, from that very cross he was ruling over the course of the Roman empire, and of every other nation that has arisen since or ever will be. And in carrying the cross, we are ruling with him.

Jesus came down that road because in spite of all their failures, he loved them. And the good news is that though the road to Emmaus started in tears, it ended in joy. Even if we've missed out, misunderstood or lost our way, Jesus still comes alongside us to find us and restore us. If you are on the road to Emmaus today, if you've suffered a disappointment you cannot understand, if the pain is so great you're at the screaming point and running away, if you don't know how God fits into what's been happening in your life, if it's all too much for you, then know this: *Jesus still walks this road today.* And as you invite him in to break bread with you, your eyes will be opened. It may not undo what has been done, but it will reveal something greater — the fact that he is with you.

He has a plan for your life. Every place of disappointment and death can become, in his hands, an opportunity for resurrection.

REFLECTIONS FOR DISCUSSION:

How do you understand disillusionment? How often have you experienced it? Has this chapter helped you to see how you may have set yourself up for disappointment? Has your experience of disillusionment blinded you to things God was doing in your life? Try going back and re-evaluating!

This chapter talks about how the revelation of Biblical truth led to a revelation of Jesus and in an instant changed the perspective and lives of these disciples. Has this ever happened to you? What does it say about the supernatural way God uses the Bible to change our lives? And what does it tell us about the fact you can't really know and encounter Jesus fully without submitting to the Scriptures?

CHAPTER 11

FINDING JESUS IN THE VALLEY OF TEARS

Philip Logan

How much can the events of one day so radically change the direction of the rest of your life? direction of the rest of your life. I have had two of these days in recent years.

The first was on the morning of the 20th of November 2011, when I begrudgingly accepted an invitation to go to church. I was 27 years old, with wild dreadlocked hair and filled with anger. I walked into the meeting, which was held in a dated hotel function room in Newcastle, England. That day, the Holy Spirit took hold of me, and I walked to the altar trembling from the power that seemed to be surging through my body. Knowing my life was a hopeless mess, I asked Jesus Christ to be my Lord and Savior. Meeting Jesus was the most wonderful thing that could have ever happened to me. He came into my life with such power, and changed me into a different person. He poured his love into me, flooding my heart with his grace. The rubble left from where I had blown up my life with drugs and toxic relationships was washed away in seconds, making their memories seem like a fading bad dream. I could no long relate to the person I had been. I could never go back. The difference in me was like night and day. I had so much gratitude towards Jesus for saving me, I could see no other option but to spend my life following him. The revelation that was cemented in my heart from the beginning was that Jesus is a God who saves. His goodness is astounding! He is a God of power whom we can encounter and whose voice we can hear. These simple but profound revelations were crucial to getting me through the years that would follow.

The second day that altered the course of my life happened seven months later in a hospital room on the other side of the world in Wellington, New Zealand, when I was diagnosed with cancer. The day began like most days. I went to work and during the morning, I began to feel a little off color. Within a few hours, I was checking myself into a hospital with agonizing stomach cramps and a high fever. This led to emergency surgery for what was a suspected appendicitis. I woke up in agony from the surgery to the news that my appendix had ruptured during the procedure and torn a hole in my bowel releasing toxins into my body. That night, I was deathly ill. The next day some very serious looking doctors approached my bed, with a grave look on their faces, and informed me that I had cancer and that I urgently needed to go straight back into the operating theatre. I had just enough time to phone England, where it was the middle of the night, to tell my parents, before I was back in surgery again. This was the traumatic beginning of what would become a long battle with this evil disease.

Even though I was young in my faith, only having walked with the Lord for seven months, I knew this sickness was not God's will. I didn't get angry at him or blame him. Instead in my weakness, I thrust myself into his arms. I fully expected him to heal me "from the word go." Why? Because the God I had come to know saves and heals.

After recovering from the surgery, I returned to England to undergo chemotherapy. The treatment was brutal, and caused me to be extremely ill. The effects of the drugs caused my skin to sting and my limbs to ache. I was bound to my bed for nearly two weeks after each dose. It even hurt to cry, and was truly a miserable state to be in. Still, I pressed into the Lord as best I knew how. Instead of numbing my soul with television, I chose to worship and feed myself with his truth. On better days, I would spend hours ministering to the Lord on my guitar, playing him simple songs and heartfelt psalms. His presence was so close during those days, and brought respite from the distress of the treatment. I learned to find strength by latching onto his heart in worship.

About four months into this ordeal, my oncologist made the decision to stop the treatment because my body was rejecting the drug so severely. I was so relieved to put it behind me, and was determined to believe that this must be the end of the fight. However, it was only a few short months later before I was back in the hospital with severe abdominal pain. For the next eight months, I was frequenting hospital, being admitted for days at a time, with the same awful pain and vomiting. It would often occur at night time and we'd have to call an ambulance to take me to the emergency room. I had several scans and x-rays through this time which always came back inconclusive. This was a testing season, and I found it particularly hard not having answers, while repeatedly undergoing the same painful attacks, which began to get more and more frequent.

For the most part of that year, I had managed by his grace to bear up under the weight of the darkness that seemed to be pressing in on me so heavily. However one night, late in the summer of 2013, I was lying in bed when this excruciating pain began again. It felt like a knife twisting in my gut. It was the worst it had ever been to date. All that day I had been meditating on Psalm 23:1, which (in the Passion paraphrase) proclaims God as our fierce protector. I started speaking this truth out, trying to focus on Jesus and not on the pain. At that moment, I had this demonically inspired thought: "If God is my fierce protector, why isn't he protecting me now?" Usually, I'd be able to fend off such an accusation but in that moment, it seemed to steal my trust in God. At this point, despair filled my heart and I started screaming at God: "Why won't you heal me? Why are you letting this happen to me?"

It wasn't too long after that I had a different type of scan. The image showed my gut lit up like a Christmas tree, revealing a mass of cancer wrapped around my intestine. This had grown in exactly the same spot as my previous surgery, making it extremely difficult to distinguish from scar tissue on the previous scans. I had lost so much weight by this point I was just skin and bone. Eventually, my intestine was completely strangled shut by the disease. I could no longer eat as nothing could pass through. I was again rushed to the hospital and put on the list for emergency surgery.

I was so weak and discouraged by this point. God felt so distant from me. I felt so hurt and disappointed that he hadn't healed me, and that the suffering was so ruthless. I didn't walk away from him, but I did harden my heart. His goodness became so hard to see. I lay in my hospital bed waiting for my surgery riddled with fear, and a plague of negative thoughts swirled around my mind. No longer could I muster up the strength to fight them off, so I just yielded to them, fully aware that it was the enemy. I felt defeated and left for dead.

I was told by my surgeon prior to the operation that he wasn't sure if there was anything he could do for me. His concern was that he might find cancerous nodules all over the wall of my abdomen, forcing him to just have to sew me back up again and sealing me in that condition. They were hard words to bear as I was headed to the operating theatre. I drifted off to sleep, listening to the countdown of the anesthetist and not knowing in what condition I would wake in, or if I would awake at all.

Incredibly, and to the credit of my amazing surgeon and the many people praying around the world, I awoke to the news that the surgery was a success. He found several tumors, but was able to remove each of them, as well as the infected section of bowel, and join it all up again.

After the surgery I was extremely weak, having barely eaten for the month prior to the operation. I got strong enough in the hospital to get discharged. However, when I got home, my condition rapidly deteriorated. I had no strength left. I weighed around 55kg (122 pounds), and I felt I was on the verge of death. It's a strange feeling to have so little life in your body. Every time I shut my eyes, it felt like it could be the last time. My parents remained positive in my presence, but they told me some time later that they would be before God night after night pleading with him to spare my life.

At this time I felt so wrapped in darkness I had no hope. I couldn't feel the presence of God or hear his voice like I once could. I would ponder on the things that I had always desired: a wife, children, taking the gospel to the nations, but at this time felt like they could never happen. I knew if I died I would get to be with Jesus, but it was tragic feeling the thought of not ever getting to experience those things I so wanted in this lifetime.

It was one night around this time that the Lord came to me in a dream. This may sound strange to you, but I'm recording it just as I experienced it. I saw myself lying in a hospital bed, and he came walking up to my bedside. His countenance was so warm and inviting, with eyes full of love and a gentle smile. Extraordinarily, he seemed to be dressed as a doctor and, as my dream continued, he began to examine me. Using an otoscope, he looked into my ears. He peered in and, just as if he were my family physician, gave the diagnosis in a warm, playful tone of voice: "Now then, someone hasn't been oiling their ears". He then bent down and blew into my ear, and immediately out of my mouth (in the dream), I spat out thick black wax. I woke from the dream, knowing that God had opened my ears to hear him again. Everything began to change after this encounter, and physically I began to get stronger. Someone once told me God speaks to people in dreams sometimes because they are unable or even unwilling to hear him in their conscious minds. That would certainly fit me in this instance. It also explains how Jesus so often seems to come to people in the Muslim world who otherwise could never hear the gospel. But that's a digression!

A short time later I was invited to attend a conference. Although I was still very weak, I felt God wanted me to go. At the event, the Holy Spirit was moving powerfully. Many people were being touched significantly by the Lord, but I felt numb to what was happening. At one point during a ministry time, I heard a lady say these simple words over the microphone: "I feel like God wants to restore trust in the room right now." As soon as these words came out of her mouth, I fell to my knees as the love of God poured into my heart. I began wailing and sobbing, as he lovingly restored my trust toward him. Before that moment I had felt so broken inside, but I came out of that encounter renewed in my love for him and the courage to follow him wholeheartedly once more. I ended the week feeling physically strengthened.

I knew that now I was starting to feel better, conversations regarding chemotherapy would soon emerge and I was terrified. The very thought of going through that suffering again tormented me. Sure enough, a date was set to begin treatment that December. Everything in me wanted to refuse it. I needed to know what God was saying.

Some of the best advice I have ever been given for when we are desperate for a word from God is to open up the Psalms. Then plow your way through, one Psalm after another, until he speaks and you feel his breath upon the words you are reading. So that day I sat cross-legged on the floor and read page after page, waiting on him. Finally, I came to Psalm 84:5-7, "Blessed are those whose strength is in you, in whose heart are the highways to Zion. As they go through the valley of Baca [tears] they make it a place of springs; the early rain also covers it with pools. They go from strength to strength; each one appears before God in Zion."

I had my promise! I knew what God was saying for the season ahead. He was going to meet me along the way, taking me through the valley of tears and turning my tears into blessing, enabling me to go from strength to strength. With his voice speaking to me through his Word came hope.

Even so, I still had a nagging sense of fear about the treatment. I know what I am writing may seem strange to some, but I can only relate what happened as best I can. The night before chemo was about to begin, the Lord came to me again in my sleep. In the dream, I stood before a man who beamed with affection towards me. I was sure it was the Lord. He asked me: "What are your dreams for the future?" I was furious that he could ask me such a question in my present situation, and I yelled at him with tears streaming down my face: "How can you ask me about the future, when I don't know if I'm going to be alive in six months time? Don't you know I'm about to start chemotherapy again in the morning?" But he just looked at me lovingly, ignored my question and gently repeated his: "What are your dreams for the future?" In that moment, I felt courageous hope fill my heart and permission to dream beyond cancer. I then began to tell the Lord all the dreams that I'd lost hope for. I woke up, knowing that I was going to live and see my dreams fulfilled.

The beginning of chemo was very hard. My hair fell out. I felt sick, achy and tired. But I stood on the word he gave me. I declared it and sang it until it became part of me. For the first months, it looked much like I had got it all wrong. The cumulative effect of the drug over subsequent treatments was making me weaker. But then something began to happen. I started to have these incredible encounters with God as I discovered the place of refreshing he had talked to me about in Psalm 84:6.

In the months that followed, I went to conferences up and down the length and breadth of England. One conference in London was a healing school at which the speaker was Randy Clark. It wasn't easy finding the courage to travel all the way from the Scottish borders while feeling so unwell, and at a point in my treatment cycle when even catching a cold could be very dangerous. On the day I was to travel, I sat waiting at the train station feeling vulnerable and pondering on my fears. I looked up into the sky and I saw two of the most unusual clouds I've ever seen. One looked just like a feather and the other a set of wings, I stared in amazement at these clouds and wondered if maybe God was speaking to me. Moments later I received a text message from a friend saying this: "I was just praying for you and I felt like God gave me Psalm 91:4 for you: 'He shall cover you with his pinions [feathers], and under his wings you will find refuge; his faithfulness is a shield and buckler.'" I sat there in awe as it seemed that God himself had formed clouds just to speak to me! After that, I went to the conference in full assurance I was supposed to be there. I received a powerful touch from the Holy Spirit that week. Among the many ways he blessed me was by healing my intestine from a horrible issue that had been troubling me greatly since the surgery.

I had so many extraordinary encounters through that six months of chemo, too many to write about here. The amazing thing was that about half way through treatment, I started to feel stronger and my hair started to grow in thicker. To the amazement of my nurses who administered the drug, this continued to happen through the remainder of my treatment. This is totally contrary to the usual cumulative effects of the drug, where you typically get weaker and sicker throughout. However, I ended my six months with a full head of hair and barely any side-effects. A few days after my last treatment, I was out digging in the garden and felt completely healthy as if none of it had ever happened.

When I look back over that season, there were indeed many tears in the dark valley. But when I got to the end of that course of chemo and looked back along the road, I didn't see the pain. All I saw was the good he did along the way. He opened my eyes to him as the loving Father that he is, the One who is there walking every step with me (Psalm 121). Through that time, he built in my heart a solid trust that with him I can walk through the hardest situations. The truth is his goodness far outweighs any pain we can endure. The goodness of God extends far beyond and above what we read in the pages of the Bible. What is written in the Bible is meant to become real in our lives today. It was not just for then! The experiences we read about in one sense can only be truly and fully understood as we ourselves live them and meet God in our own hard places.

I'm so thankful for that part of my journey because I learned the power of a God-given promise. I learned how when we stand on his Word, our circumstances have to bend their knee to King Jesus. This saying is true: "Do not let your circumstances dictate where you are going. Instead, direct your circumstances to where you are going." This is what the word of the Lord does. When we know what he is saying, we can steer our circumstances toward his will in prayer and declaration (1 Jn. 5:14-15). It's one of the extraordinary privileges that comes with being a child of God.

I've found that discouragement comes when I look to myself. The reason is simple. My strength and ability apart from him is always going to come up short when my world is falling apart. There have been many times when I've wondered if this is happening to me because I don't have enough faith. This thought is never helpful, because it pulls our eyes from him and looks to what is within ourselves rather than to the Lord. Faith is not something I can conjure up. It's a gift that comes from my relationship with Christ. I found that my faith grows in direct proportion to how well I get to know his heart and nature. The greater the revelation of his goodness I carry in my heart, the greater my ability to trust and believe that his intentions toward me are always good. The promises that he gives us in bad times often don't match our present circumstances. They are our destination at the end of the valley, our road map to get us through. It takes courage to believe them, particularly when their fulfillment is prolonged.

I would love to say that my journey with cancer ended there but unfortunately, I can't say that just yet. Not long after I finished chemo, I was diagnosed with *pseudomyxoma peritonei*, which is a very rare form of cancer that forms within the peritoneum (abdominal cavity). In August 2015, I underwent 9 hours of specialist surgery to remove diseased sections of my bowel, liver, diaphragm and peritoneum. I spent nearly three weeks in the hospital recovering, and following this I went through another six months of chemo.

Then in September 2016, it was discovered that I had two tumors in my right lung and one in the pleural cavity. For the first time in all these years fighting, I was told that I was terminal and offered no curative treatment. I remember leaving the hospital that day crushed by the news. I went for a walk along the beach trying to process and find some clarity in my thoughts. I could feel that familiar cloud of doubt and confusion start to pull me down. I kept muttering desperately, "God what are you saying?" as I watched my feet stomp through the dusty sand. All of a sudden, these words came cutting through my mind: "God is not a man, that he should lie." I felt like my head was pulled above the water and in that moment I could breathe again. I started declaring: "God you're not a liar! I know what you've spoken to me, this can't be the way! I know you're not a liar!"

"God is not man, that he should lie, or a son of man, that he should change his mind. Has he said, and will he not do it? Or has he spoken, and will he not fulfill it?" (Num. 23:19).

In the months that followed, I'd love to say that I felt full of faith and joy. However, this was probably one of the most difficult periods of my life. I felt exhausted and stretched. Each day felt like trudging through mud. There were days when I screamed, swore and sobbed as I scrabbled to find language for the turmoil I felt inside. I gathered people around, and we prayed and pressed into the Lord often. I eventually came to the conclusion that I wasn't going to accept any treatment if it wasn't curative; that if God said he was going to heal me, radiotherapy to prolong my life wasn't the answer.

It was one morning shortly after this that out of the blue I received a phone call from my oncologist. He told me that a surgeon in London had reviewed my case, and thought that he could do the surgery I needed. Incredibly, this man went on to perform an operation that quite possibly no one else in England could pull off, saving my life once again. God is faithful.

At the time of writing, I still can't say with complete certainty that it's over. But I know what God has said, and therefore I know what He is going to do. I know I will live to glorify God for the fulfillment of his promise of salvation in this lifetime. I choose to keep my eyes fixed on Jesus, and drink in the goodness of who he is. That's where I find the strength, hope and the courage to continue to keep believing, as I walk towards the promised land.

I have had so many doors of opportunity open up to over the last five years. I've shared the gospel in hospitals, prisons, churches and on the streets. I've seen many people come to Jesus. It's not hard for me to see the fruit that has come from the past five years. I am the man I am today because of it. I believe the only reason I'm still alive is because I continually said yes to Jesus; the rest has all been down to him. I don't know why I have had to go through all of this, and why I'm not yet healed fully. But what I do know is this: he is forever faithful, wholly good and always my glorious Savior.

Early on in my journey, I had a dream in which the Lord directed me to declare Isa. 62:11 every day. I remember waking excitedly from the dream, hurriedly reaching to find my Bible to see what the Scripture said. My heart gasped in hope as I read these words, "Behold, the Lord has proclaimed to the end of the earth: Say to the daughter of Zion, 'Behold, your salvation comes; behold, his reward is with him, and his recompense before him.'" To this day I stand on these words. Surely my salvation is coming!

So here is my counsel to you. If you ever find yourself in the dark valley of tears as I have, hold on, fear not and trust him, because where others will find only pain, you will find Jesus. And finding him is worth the price of every tear you could ever shed.

Philip Logan went to be with his Lord January 6, 2018 at his home in Wooler, Northumberland, England, surrounded by his family and friends. He was 33 years old. He is survived by his parents Hugh and Margaret.

CHAPTER 12

LIFE IN THE REFINER'S FIRE

"Great faith is the product of great fights. Great testimonies are the outcome of great tests. Great triumphs can only come out of great trials."
Smith Wigglesworth

For Philip Logan, the valley of tears became the place where he encountered the Refiner's fire. He found a faith more precious than gold. That faith carried him eventually into the presence of the Lord, and I am only one person among many who can witness to the fact he lived for Christ until the day the Lord took him home, a day on which he was surrounded by close friends praying through the hours of his last night on earth. God was glorified in his death as in his life. Gold, as part of this material world, will one day perish, even though it has been tested and made perfect in the fire. But our faith will never perish. And this is what Peter teaches us at the beginning of his first letter.

The letter is written to a suffering church. So it's significant that Peter starts it off with a declaration of praise, "Blessed be the God and Father of our Lord Jesus Christ!" (1 Pet. 1:3). Whether we like it or not, as is abundantly illustrated in Philip's story, life involves suffering. The world approaches the possibility of suffering with dread. No Christian would deny the pain of suffering or welcome it with open arms, but there is a critical difference between the believer and the non-believer. Jesus had given Peter a personal prophecy that he would die a martyr's death. He lived his whole Christian life in that certain knowledge, yet he refused to allow it to hinder his serving the Lord. In making this declaration of praise, he was asserting the monumental fact that God is greater than anything that may happen to us, and that we can trust him to look after us in the midst of it. Whatever else happens, I will bless the Lord. Whatever I feel like, I will bless the Lord. My act of blessing God is an expression of my determination to follow him, no matter what my outward circumstances may be.

I believe God understands the feelings we go through in times of trial. I believe he knows our ups and downs. He doesn't expect us to glide through trouble, and he doesn't condemn us when we waver. But something in our spirit has to take hold of faith in God at a very fundamental level, in a determination that we will not allow the bad things that happen to us to separate us from the Lord or stop us from following him. Our discipleship is proven real only when it is tested. Great triumphs can only come out of great tests, as Wigglesworth said.

Jesus is described here as Lord and Christ. Christ means Messiah. He is our great deliverer, our hope, God's immeasurable gift to us. Yet he is equally our Lord. Many want to know Jesus as deliverer, as the one who does things for us. *But as surely as he delivers us from something, he delivers us into something.* What we are delivered into is his lordship. Christianity works through submission. Why? Because God has built order into creation. Where there is order, there is authority, and where there is authority, there is submission. God is our ruler, not our facilitator. He is our Lord, not our life coach. Many people today think the opposite of order is freedom. That is a lie. The opposite of order is chaos. *Order releases freedom within boundaries God has set.* For the Christian, the most fundamental fact is that Jesus is Lord. Our allegiance to him is tested and refined in times of suffering. Are we willing to follow him when times are hard as much as when times are good?

"According to his great mercy," Peter continues, "he has caused us to be born again to a living hope." The basis of all God's dealings with us is his mercy. His anger against human sin and rebellion was visited on his own Son so that we might be saved. In times of suffering we need to keep this fact in front of us. Our emotions may be screaming that God has forgotten us. But that is all the more reason to stand firm in our spirit in the declaration that God is for us. And he proved that when he sent his own Son to die for us. The fact is that even God's discipline is an expression of his mercy. He may allow us to lose the false supports we have built around ourselves if those supports are preventing us from accessing his truer and greater strength instead. There should never be a single moment when we forget what he did for us. The determination to give thanks, no matter what we feel like, will save us from the bitterness that brings nothing but death. And the more we live every moment in awareness of God's mercy, the more that mercy will flow through us. People long for the touch of God's mercy. Just let that mercy flow through you.

And we have a "living hope." Our hope is not dead. It was born in an empty tomb. It comes "through the resurrection of Jesus Christ from the dead." Even when you run out of hope, God does not. Hope is what keeps us going when things are hard. And our hope is not a product of what we feel like. All of us have days when things seem very bleak, but Jesus will never fail you. Even if he comes to you at the screaming point, as N.T. Wright puts it, he will come. Just because you're desperate doesn't mean you're out of hope. *Hope is a lifeline God throws to you in your desperation.* Hope assures us he is with us. When you're at the end of your tether, ask him for that lifeline. Ask him to give you something just to show you that he's still with you. Even a small sign can bring enormous comfort.

Hope is powerful because it directs us to something bigger than our feelings. Hope points us to "an inheritance that is imperishable, undefiled, and unfading, kept in heaven for you, who by God's power are being guarded through faith for a salvation ready to be revealed in the last time" (verse 5). The word "guarded" refers to a military encampment, and that is what God has placed around us. The same word occurs in Philippians. The believers were suffering because of their faith (Phil. 1:29-30), and they needed reassurance. Paul told them to pray and not to be anxious, and that the peace of God that passes all understanding would "keep" (= place a military guard around) their hearts and minds in Christ (Phil. 4:7).

It's hard for us sometimes to comprehend the reality of this protection. But it's real. In his vision of the heavenly throne room, John saw two groups of angelic beings described as elders and living creatures, whose job was to present the prayers of suffering saints before God (Rev. 5:8). He also saw how angels were assigned on behalf of each church to represent them before God and presumably to fight in the heavenly realms on their behalf (Revelation 2-3). This is only part of the military garrison God places around us. It explains why Christians have been willing to give their lives rather than compromise. It explains why, for the rest of us, we find strength to make it through rather than sinking in our suffering.

A pastor I knew once had a glimpse into this eternal realm of protection. He was driving on a remote road in northern Ontario and suddenly without warning saw an incredibly tall man in blindingly white clothing standing in the middle of the road. He screamed to a halt and the man disappeared. Shaken, he got out of his car to look for the man only to see a massive rock slide had completely washed out the road ahead of him. He was within meters of plunging down a steep cliff to his death. Other friends had a similar encounter. The husband was very ill and unable to work. Finances became desperate. One night, a knock came at the door. Two men in trench coats were standing on the doorstep and handed the wife a brown paper bag. As she began to close the door, she noticed the bag was stuffed with money. Instantly, she pulled the door back open, but the men were gone. In a street of British "terraced" houses, she could see at least a hundred meters in either direction. In a couple of seconds, the men had vaporized, but the money hadn't. It kept them until her husband recovered. God's protection is invisible, but it is not unreal.

All this leads up to the practical application Peter is making, "In this you rejoice, though now for a little while, if necessary, you have been grieved by various trials, so that the genuineness of your faith — more precious than gold that perishes though it is tested by fire — may be found to result in praise and glory and honor at the revelation of Jesus Christ" (verses 6-7). I have to confess I'm not sure I understand exactly what is involved here in the command to rejoice. I don't think he's referring to the emotion we feel when something wonderful has happened. I'm not sure how I could ever get to a place in God where I would be ecstatic about suffering. But maybe he means something a little different. Maybe he's telling us that in times of difficulty the only place you will be able to find real strength is in your relationship with the Lord. Paul talks at length about comfort coming to him in the midst of suffering (2 Cor. 1:4-7). Maybe he's showing us that God's comfort is our lifeline to make it through. To rejoice in this context may mean nothing more nor less than the ability to give thanks to God in the knowledge that what he has given us is always more than anything this world can throw at us.

Peter's phrase "if necessary" requires two things to be said about it. First, the expression in Greek refers to an action of God. What is necessary comes from God. This does not mean that God sends sickness, rejection, sorrow or pain. But it does mean that he is sovereign in it. Whenever the devil, his agents, people or circumstances are conspiring against us, God is sovereignly superintending the whole process. What he allows, he allows only to bring a greater good out of it. Our comfort is simply in knowing that he is always in control. Nothing is meaningless. The second thing about "if necessary" is that there is another, unspoken phrase: "if it is *not* necessary." Suffering is not all there is to the Christian life. There are times when we suffer, and there are times when we do not. But God uses suffering for a particular purpose. It tests our faith. Our faith is compared in this passage to gold. Both pass through the fire and are refined. Gold is the most precious material substance known to humanity. But faith is more valuable yet. Sad to say, our faith is not refined by happiness, by prosperity, by the praise of people, by the easy life. Faith, like gold, is only refined by fire. How important it is to remember that God is in the refining fire. In fact, God *is* the refining fire. When you're in the fire, remember that the Refiner is in control. *The purposes of God, no matter what it looks and feels like, are always constructive.* He may destroy things you have put ahead of him, but only because those things will ultimately fail you. He replaces them not with other things, but with a deeper knowledge of himself.

And this faith results in glory and honor at the revelation of Jesus Christ (verse 7). Peter may be talking primarily about the Lord's return, but even in this life, particularly when you have passed through the fire and remained faithful, there is a revelation of Jesus Christ. That revelation takes place in you. And I think it's in those moments, when Jesus comes to you, that the joy Peter talks about bursts forth, "Though you do not now see him, you believe in him and rejoice with joy that is inexpressible and filled with glory" (verse 9).

Out of the deep apparent hopelessness of the cross came that amazing moment of inexpressible and glorious joy when the stranger on the beach called out to the fishermen, and Peter said, "It is the Lord!" Trials come into our lives, and sometimes they are times of deep pain. But at the end of them, the moment comes when we see him again, when we recognize he never left us, when we understand how he kept us, when we say, "It is the Lord!"

Life in the Refiner's fire is never comfortable, but in the end it is always worth it. Passing through his fire is the only way to know the Refiner and to experience his limitless joy, his infinite mercy and his inexhaustible love.

In this room, in this place
You're changing me
In this heart, unfolding mysteries
In this time, in this space
Restoring things
Spirit come and speak in every heart

Lord I know that You're here and I'm lost in wonder
Here I'm held in Your love
Here and I don't want to leave this place
Lord I know that Your touch is unlike all others

Jesus temple of grace
Here and I cannot leave unchanged

In Your presence I'm refined
In Your mercy raised to life
Jesus all consuming fire have Your way

(c) Ken Riley 2015 Used by permission

REFLECTIONS FOR DISCUSSION:

Christianity works through submission. What does this mean for you? If Christ is Savior, he must be Lord. Do you agree? How does a true understanding of submission help us in relation to experiencing suffering?

What does it mean to take hold of God in our spirit? Have you ever experienced this and what kind of breakthrough did it bring for you?

Discuss an experience where you felt you went through the Refiner's fire and emerged with more gold in your faith than before.

CHAPTER 13

KEEPING FAITH THROUGH THE FIRE

Paul faced a series of enormous challenges in his life. Not many of us could write words like this, "With far greater labors, far more imprisonments, with countless beatings, and often near death. Five times I received at the hand of the Jews the forty lashes less one. Three times I was beaten with rods. Once I was stoned. Three times I was shipwrecked; a night and a day I was adrift at sea; on frequent journeys, in danger from rivers, danger from robbers, danger from my own people, danger from Gentiles, danger in the city, danger in the wilderness, danger at sea, danger from false brothers; in toil and hardship, through many a sleepless night, in hunger and thirst, often without food, in cold and exposure. And, apart from other things, there is the daily pressure on me of my anxiety for all the churches" (2 Cor. 11:23-28).

Through these trials, Paul found several powerful things to be true. These truths enabled him to come out the other end of his suffering with his faith not destroyed but strengthened. If we can learn from one man's walk with God, we will find secrets which will anchor us when the going gets tough. We will keep a perspective on faith and hope, no matter how severe or prolonged the trial. According to our limited understanding, experiencing adversity and the strengthening of our faith are opposed to each other. But such is not the case! Our faith, if we find God in it, is actually strengthened through trial.

As we look at the lessons God taught Paul, there is one thing we need to remember. The reality of our faith does not depend on outward circumstances changing or on our various needs being met, but on a revelation of the Holy Spirit to our hearts and minds of who God is, and that he is more than enough.

"But we have this treasure in jars of clay, to show that the surpassing power belongs to God and not to us" (2 Cor. 4:7). Here in one sentence is expressed the secret of the release of the power of God. God's destiny for us is to carry his power, the treasure of his presence. But we are to carry it in jars of clay. Clay pots were the humblest form of kitchenware in those days. They were cheap and unattractive. Their greatest value was the food they held within them. The paradox of the gospel is that power is released through humility and adversity.

Paul does not make this statement to suggest that we are worthless to God. He makes it to point out that in ourselves, we are nothing. However, we do have the capacity to carry something great. The prerequisite for carrying that greatness is to know that the source of that greatness is God and not us. To carry this treasure brings great joy and great pain. The greatest treasure of all is the cross. Jesus knew he was carrying the treasure when he hung on the cross. And he is our example. God exhorts us to run the race set before us, because Jesus endured the cross for the joy that was set before him. The race will at times be hard and painful, but we can run the race even as he did. You cannot carry the treasure without carrying the cross. But in the end it is always worth it.

The greatest Biblical illustration of this is the life of Mary. She was a clay pot who knew she was nothing without God, but laid her life at his feet. As a result, she was able literally to carry within her the life of God himself. And there was a cost. Not only was there the derision and social exclusion that came from being an apparently unwed mother. There was a greater pain to come, as Simeon prophesied when he met Mary in the temple, "A sword will pierce through your own soul also" (Lk. 2:35). That pain came as, many years later, Mary stood at the foot of her son's cross. Yet the joy that followed was greater, when on the third day she stood among the company of believers witnessing his resurrection.

All of us want to experience the power of God. Who would not want to prophesy, pray for the sick and see them healed, or witness miracles? But what about the cost? What does it look like to carry God's presence, his call and his destiny in the clay jars of our lives?

Paul was at a time of great crisis in his life when he wrote 2 Corinthians. According to chapter 1, the affliction was so severe it caused him to despair even of life, to feel that the sentence of death had been passed on him. Yet this is the man who in chapter 11 of the same letter mentions the signs and wonders and mighty works God had done through him, and who describes his experience of being caught up to the third heaven. The letter also tells us the same man was rejected and abandoned by the people he had led to Christ, and in whose presence all these mighty works had been done. Most pain is caused by people, and the greatest pain is caused by people we love.

Paul describes here what it means to carry the treasure in jars of clay. The bottom line is this: no matter how bad things seem or how hopeless our situation looks, God is still with us, and he will bring us through. It was through suffering that the apostle learned the following priceless lessons. Let him share the treasure with you.

1. THERE IS AN END TO EVERY VALLEY
(2 COR. 4:8-9)

At a time of great crisis in his life, Paul described his situation with four parallel word pictures. Each of these reminds us that no matter how bad things seem or how hopeless our situation looks, God is still there with us, and he will bring an end to our suffering.

"Afflicted in every way, but not crushed." The first phrase translates the Greek word for "tribulation," meaning a severe trial or affliction. The second word means "to be crushed, as in a narrow defile." Paul had walked many narrow mountain passes. One he would have been particularly familiar with was near his home town of Tarsus. The picture he is drawing for us is of a traveler passing through one such place, expecting to be crushed but finding that somehow God provides a way through. Sometimes suffering appears to us like being on a dead-end street with no way out. We may feel we are being crushed by our circumstances. We will face tribulation, whatever that may look like for each of us. Yet we know the Lord is faithful. He has always provided a way through for his people. And he will for you.

"Perplexed, but not driven to despair." These words are closely related, the first speaking of despair, and the other of an utter despair with no hope. If the first pair of phrases show us a dead end street, the second pair gives us a picture of darkness surrounding us. Loss of hope leads to perplexity. Why did God allow this? Where is God in my suffering? What is going to happen to me? Such perplexity can easily lead on to depression and fear. In his relationship with the Corinthians, which had given rise to this crisis in Paul's life, the answers to these questions did not come easily. He went through an agonizing process, yet in it God strengthened him sufficiently that his perplexity did not lead to total hopelessness. Even in the darkness, God shone a light. Even when our questions are not answered, God is still there. He is greater than our questions, and his light is greater than our darkness. Paul had learned this truth, and it kept him in the time of trial.

"Persecuted, but not forsaken." The first word refers to being hunted or chased. We may feel we are being hunted like an animal. But we will never be forsaken. We may be hunted, but we will not be caught!

"Struck down, but not destroyed." The first word means to be knocked to the ground. The second word is the same one Paul uses to refer to those on their way to eternal damnation. The picture here is of a fighter bloodied and wounded, down on the canvas, yet somehow able to get back up. One translator phrased it this way, "knocked down, but not knocked out." No matter how many blows we may take, the enemy will not prevail.

2. THERE IS A POINT TO OUR SUFFERING
(2 COR. 4:10-12)

"Always carrying in the body the death of Jesus, so that the life of Jesus may also be manifested in our bodies. For we who live are always being given over to death for Jesus' sake, so that the life of Jesus also may be manifested in our mortal flesh. So death is at work in us, but life in you." Paul states that he carries around in his body the "death" of Jesus (verse 10). This word (*nekrosis*) is not the usual word he uses regarding Jesus' death, which is *thanatos*. The difference is this. *Nekrosis* refers to the *process of dying*. *Thanatos* refers to the simple *act* or *fact of dying*. Paul means that his life as a whole has been characterized by a continual dying. This dying becomes particularly evident and real in times of difficulty. There is no point denying the reality of our suffering. Suffering is a consequence of the fact we still live in a fallen world. As Christians, we are delivered from the eternal consequences of our sin, yet in this world we are by no means perfected. God protects us from all manner of things, some of which we are not even aware of. Yet his protection is primarily spiritual in nature. The results of sin are like nuclear fallout — they are experienced by the just and the unjust alike. In addition to our general exposure to life in a fallen world, God calls us in addition to be willing to suffer as Christians. It is part of the life Jesus calls us to, even as it was a part of his life on earth. Paul even says this, "In my flesh I am filling up what is lacking in Christ's afflictions for the sake of his body, that is, the church" (Col. 1:24). In the Corinthian church, the false teachers opposing Paul boasted that God's strength was manifested in their great preaching and strength of personality. Suffering was something to be despised. But Paul knew that in truth God's strength is shown just as it was at Calvary — in the weakness and vulnerability of those who place their trust in him and not in themselves. Only in this way can God be truly glorified.

It is significant that the verb "given over" in verse 11 is the same word used in the Gospels to describe Jesus' being given over to the Romans. It is actually God who has caused Paul to be given over to this dying, even though the actions of sinful people are at work in it. In the same way, God caused his Son to be given over to death for our sake. God is at work in our suffering. In a perfect world, there would be no suffering. And it was not God who ruined the perfection of the world he created us to enjoy. However, in a fallen world, God will use suffering to accomplish his purposes. But what is God's purpose in our suffering? The purpose is stated here very clearly, and repeated for emphasis. It is that the life of Jesus may be manifested or revealed in us, even in our mortal bodies, which is the very place we are suffering. How is the life of Jesus revealed in us through suffering? There are two ways: *inward* and *outward*.

Inwardly, God is refining us. Peter spoke of a faith which is proven genuine because it is refined by fire (1 Pet. 1:7). God is removing the dross or false dependencies from our life. All too often, we depend on the wrong things for happiness — money, job, reputation, health and so on. There is nothing wrong with these things, unless they become a substitute or idol which we seek instead of God alone. God will remove those human supports if they stand in the way of a deeper walk with him. This is the discipline of sonship which seems hard at the time, but later on produces a harvest of righteousness (Heb. 12:7-11). God may be refining us by making us more dependent on him alone in times there is simply nowhere else to go. Paul states this quite clearly, "For we were so utterly burdened beyond our strength that we despaired of life itself. Indeed, we felt that we had received the sentence of death. But this was to make us rely not on ourselves but on God who raises the dead" (2 Cor. 1:8-9).

Outwardly, God is causing us to bear more fruit. Paul says, "For we who live are always being given over to death for Jesus' sake, so that the life of Jesus also may be manifested in our mortal flesh" (verse 11). What this means is made clear in the next statement, "So death is at work in us, but life in you" (verse 12). Through the suffering that comes from our sacrificial service to God, others will be touched, perhaps in ways we are not even aware of. All that we go through has a point. How can you help people who are suffering unless you have walked through suffering yourself? And if God has helped us in our suffering, that itself is an assurance to others he will help them also. Jesus said the same thing, "Every branch that does bear fruit he prunes, that it may bear more fruit" (Jn. 15:2).

God is always investing into our lives in order that we might be more productive and fruitful. Everything he does, even things that seem painful, has a positive purpose. Even where the enemy is without doubt at work, God will sovereignly bring good out of evil. Therefore, in times of trial, remember these things. God is at work in the circumstances, accomplishing purposes we cannot yet see or understand but which are nevertheless real. He is drawing us closer to himself. And he is changing us to make us a greater blessing to others.

3. HONESTY BRINGS VICTORY (2 COR. 4:13-15)

Verse 13 brings what may be one of the most misinterpreted verses in the New Testament, "Since we have the same spirit of faith according to what has been written, 'I believed, and so I spoke,' we also believe, and so we also speak." Paul is quoting Psalm 116:10. In the faith movement, this verse has been taken to mean that in spite of his negative circumstances, Paul was able to speak forth a word of faith or a "positive confession." This confession crushed all doubt and unbelief, and changed his situation from negative to positive, having the power to move God to respond. In other words, if we have enough "faith," we can transform all negative circumstances into positive ones and thus come into victory. In an extreme form, it is claimed that our words of positive confession make us co-creators with God of the future. This surely is heresy, not so much because it unduly exalts us, but because it diminishes God. The tragic fact is that countless numbers of believers have suffered from disappointment trying (and failing) to manufacture this kind of faith.

Let's take a closer look at Psalm 116. To begin with, the psalmist does not speak a "positive confession" which denies the reality of what is going on. On the contrary, he acknowledges just how awful his situation is, "The snares of death encompassed me.... I suffered distress and anguish. Then I called on the name of the Lord: 'O Lord, I pray, deliver my soul!'" (Ps. 116:3-4). Then a few verses later, he cries out the words quoted by Paul, "I believed, even when I spoke, 'I am greatly afflicted.'" (Ps.

116:10). His words to God are not a declaration of great victory, but one of great desperation. Yet they are nonetheless words of great faith. He maintained his faith in God, while at the same time acknowledging the severity of his situation. He did not rise up triumphantly with words of faith which vaporized the dangers he was facing. He knew, in fact, that he had no ability whatever to change his situation. Nor was he under the mistaken belief that God is obligated to comply with our prayers when they are uttered in a certain manner. He knew he was helpless in the face of adversity, and cried out to God for mercy, knowing full well that he had no claim on God, and no right to force God to respond to his request. Yet what he did in the end was far more effective. He cast himself on God's mercy.

We will never understand how this works unless we define faith properly as personal trust born out of relationship. Faith is not a mental certainty of belief. Neither is it an emotional high. God is not obligated to respond either to our mental certainty or to our upbeat emotional state. Just because I *believe* something good will happen, or just because I *feel* something good will happen does not mean something good *will* happen! In the Bible, faith above all is the expression of personal trust in God.

The fact that our finances and personal happiness are not driven by our positive confessions may disappoint faith preachers, but it should bring a massive relief to the rest of us. Why? *Because such beliefs place an unbearable burden on us to produce something we can never make happen.* Our mental certainties may be shaken from time to time, yet that is not the foundation for our faith. Our emotions may go up and down, but that is not the basis of our faith either. The basis of our faith is in the mercy of a God who at his own unbelievable cost has reached down to save us from eternal ruin. The power of our faith is not in our words or thoughts. *The power of our faith is in his promise that he will never abandon us.* As Heb. 13:5 says, "I will never leave you nor forsake you."

The psalmist comes to God as a friend to whom he can pour out all his troubles. What good is a friend if we cannot be honest with him? Jesus told the disciples they were no longer his servants but his friends (Jn. 15:15). *It is precisely because of his faith* that he cries out to God in openness and honesty about his situation, which no amount of positive thinking or confessing or believing or feeling can change. But somewhere in the heart cry is expressed the hope that out of this mess God will bring deliverance. And this is just what happened, as we find out before the psalm concludes, "You have loosed my bonds" (Ps. 116:16).

The psalms are full of desperate and very realistic cries to God. For instance, "How long, O Lord? Will you be angry forever?" (Ps. 79:5). Or again, "For my soul is full of troubles, and my life draws near to Sheol… You have put me in the depths of the pit, in the regions dark and deep" (Ps. 88:3, 6). Or again, "How long, O Lord? Will you hide yourself forever? How long will your wrath burn like fire?" (Ps. 89:46). When we are in trouble, it is a sign of *faith*, not of *unbelief*, to acknowledge the critical nature of the situation and our own weakness and helplessness in it, and to cast ourselves instead on the mercy of God.

Religion relates to God on the basis of rules rather than relationship. It reduces faith from relational trust and dependency to the power of independent mental belief. It then tries to control God and force his response by things we do or say. Perhaps unwittingly, much faith teaching falls into this trap. Positive confession, much like the positive thinking of non-Christian motivational speakers, attempts to bury or deny hard realities we are facing, but inevitably fails in its efforts to change them, because God will not respond to manipulation. This then leads on to disillusionment and bitterness against God. We believe a lie about God, and then blame him for not changing his character to suit it.

These "faith" declarations are often attempts to extricate ourselves from painful situations we are facing, rather than submitting to the refining and pruning work of God in the midst of them. True faith, on the other hand, is born of genuine relationship with the Father, and brings our discouraging reality in utter honesty before the Lord. It allows the expression of our mental doubt and emotional anguish, but looks to God to reveal his grace as he brings answers in his own time and way. This leads us not to disillusionment and anger, but to maturity and peace.

Faith is not a psychological state in which we attempt to hype ourselves up into "believing" a certain thing — for instance to say, "I am healed," when obviously I am not. This is not to discourage us from taking a stand of faith. It is merely to acknowledge that a place of genuine faith comes against a background of human weakness and a consciousness that we are utterly helpless to bring about the conclusion we desire.

Nevertheless, such true faith concludes that God is entirely able to do anything he wants on our behalf. Not only that, but he invites us — no, he commands us! — to call on him for help. This is the strength-in-weakness faith modelled by Paul to the Corinthians. It is, incidentally, a faith which enabled him to heal the sick, to raise the dead, to win thousands to Christ and to plant the seed of the Gospel, almost single-handedly, through most of the Roman Empire in sixteen short years. Surely this faith is good enough for us!

And so Paul, identifying with the words of the Psalm, and knowing that he carries around in his own mortal flesh *both the death and the life* of Jesus (verse 10), cries out, "We also believe, and so we also speak, knowing that he who raised the Lord Jesus will raise us also..." (verses 13-14). Paul's certainty of deliverance is focused on the resurrection. We have no guarantee that, in the meantime, suffering will not continue. However, God is committed to manifesting his life in us even now in the midst of these sufferings. All this, Paul says, is "for your sake, so that as grace extends to more and more people it may increase thanksgiving, to the glory of God" (verse 15). He comes back to reminding himself again that there is outward fruit to his own suffering. The fruit is manifest in the lives of others, but ultimately and more importantly, it is to the glory of God. And in the process, Paul himself did experience deliverance, "He has delivered us from such a deadly peril, and he will deliver us" (2 Cor. 1:10). Even if our trials continue, we have the joy of knowing that they are producing a positive result in others, and thus giving glory to God. And it is not in the heart of God for us to undergo gratuitous suffering — suffering for the sake of suffering. He moves in the midst of suffering to fulfil his purposes. Suffering came into the world as a result of the fall, and God sent his Son to suffer to deliver us from that curse. Yet in this life, the deliverance is never complete. Where we cannot understand, we can still trust.

So what are to do? We are to bring our suffering to the Father. We do that in the context of a living relationship of trust in which we have already encountered the greatest deliverance we will ever find — eternal salvation. We do it in the context of a commitment to follow him no matter what may happen or how he chooses to respond to our prayers. This in itself brings a greater deliverance than anything else, for in it we find the presence of the Lord. The presence of the Lord is our greatest reward, and all through the ages God's people in suffering have found it to be the eternal weight of glory that far outweighs our present troubles (2 Cor. 4:17). At the end of the day, our relationship with the Father is the most precious thing we have. That is why our faith is focused on that relationship, rather than on the possession of anything this world may have to offer. Yet in it all, God is a loving Father. If we seek his kingdom first, he will add whatever we need (Mt. 6:33). Even as our sufferings overflow, so also does our comfort (2 Cor. 1:3-7). He will not fail us.

4. HOW YOU SEE, NOT WHAT YOU SEE
(2 COR. 4:16-18)

Paul now begins to bring his thoughts to a conclusion, "So we do not lose heart. Though our outer self is wasting away, our inner self is being renewed day by day" (verse 16). Amazingly, he is encouraged not *in spite of*, but *because of* the battles he has been describing. His mortal body is wasting away, yet at the same time his spirit is being renewed. No matter how much time I may spend at the gym, the struggles of life are ceaselessly wearing down my physical body and will eventually lead to my physical death. But the work of the Holy Spirit within me is daily strengthening my spirit and will lead me to eternal life. What good news is that! The phrase "being renewed" literally means being made *continually as good as new*. The phrase "day by day" refers to a steady progress — every day is a new advance. True renewal of spirit is found in carrying the cross. God's blessing will come to those who walk in Jesus' footsteps.

In verse 17, he says that our troubles are light and momentary, whereas the glory to come is heavy and eternal. We think of our troubles as heavy and overwhelming. Paul had every reason to think the same way. Think of the two massive lists of tribulations recorded in 2 Cor. 6:4-10 and 11:23-29! Most of us would be floored by only one or two of the many things he had to endure. But Paul sees things differently. He has in mind a picture of a scale. On the one side are our present troubles, and on the other our eternal glory. For him, his troubles are entirely outweighed by the glory that is to come. What a glory that must be!

In the face of such incredible suffering, how on earth did Paul maintain this attitude? His secret is found in verse 18, and the secret is all about *seeing*. A literal reading of the Greek yields the translation, "Our light and momentary troubles are achieving for us an eternal glory that far outweighs them all *provided that* we fix our gaze not on what is seen but on what is not seen." Whether or not our earthly troubles lead us on to an eternal glory in the way that God intends seems to depend upon how we look at them. The key to understanding Paul's meaning is in the two different words he uses for "seeing." The word we have translated "fix our gaze on" is the Greek verb *skopeo*, from which we get the word "scope," as in a telescope, microscope, or scope of a rifle. This is a highly concentrated form of vision, vision that sees what normal vision does not see. The Greek word for normal sight is *blepo*, and that is used twice in the rest of the sentence. We fix our eyes (*skopeo*) not on what is "seen" with normal vision (*blepo*) but on what is "not seen" — what normal vision cannot see. What we "fix our gaze upon" through the scope of a rifle gives us a far different and far more accurate picture of reality than what we "see" with the naked eye.

This means there are two types of vision available to us. The first sees only the superficial. The second understands what lies behind it. The first type of vision will never see past the troubles we experience to encounter the mercy and comfort of God. This will lead us to blame God and others for all the trouble in the world and in our own lives. The second type of vision understands that God himself, by sending his Son to take the punishment for our sin, endured a suffering we will never comprehend. He did so in order to redeem and make sense of the sufferings we still experience in this life, and to translate them into eternal glory by a process we can understand only by faith and trust in his goodness.

Heb. 11:1 defines this "spiritual seeing," this telescopic vision, as *faith*, "Now faith is the assurance of things hoped for, the conviction of things not seen." The things we cannot see with our natural vision can be grasped by the spiritual vision made available only through faith. Seeing from God's perspective does not answer all our questions, but it does enable us to walk through the worst situations and emerge with our faith intact, perhaps even strengthened. Seeing with natural eyes only will lead to anger and bitterness when negative things occur. We will shut ourselves off from the redemptive working of the Holy Spirit, whose desire is to turn our ashes into gold. Only if we choose to see reality from an eternal perspective will we gain God's comfort and see the bigger picture. The alternative — to fall into self-pity and despair — is ours to make. Self-pity is one of the most powerful and destructive spiritual dead-ends that exist, because it cuts us off from the love and grace of God, causes us to be bitter and angry with him and others, and denies every good thing he has done for us. Few people had more reason to choose the latter course than Paul, yet few people rejected it so strongly, and with such powerful results. Corrie ten Boom lived through the horrors of a Nazi concentration camp, yet lived to speak words that brought healing to many, "There is no pit so deep the love of God does not go deeper."

One final thing remains to be said, and cannot be assumed. The ability to see things from God's perspective — to have spiritual vision — is not something we can manufacture. It is a gift of God's grace birthed in our personal relationship with the Lord. Faith itself is a gift. It takes time to build a relationship with anyone, and God is no exception. It takes time to pray and to read the Word. It takes time to take quiet moments out, and ask for God's direction and perspective. But the price of not taking that time, of neglecting that relationship, is far too high a price to pay. We cannot allow our goals and values in life to be determined by what passes superficially before our earthly eyes. It is what does *not* appear before that lesser vision that constitutes true reality, and it is that which must fashion our life's destiny and purpose. The visible realities, like Paul's mortal body, will pass away, but the things that are unseen, like the impact of his life, will last forever. The apparent death which, on various levels, may accompany the call of God in this world is intended to bring forth a harvest of life, both in us and in those to whom we minister. This, Paul declares, is the message of the true Gospel.

REFLECTIONS FOR DISCUSSION:

Can you relate to the four figures of speech Paul uses in 2 Cor. 4:8-9, climaxing in "knocked down but not knocked out." As you look back, do these metaphors help you to process adversity you have experienced in the past? Have there been valleys you never thought you would come out of, but did?

How is it that the life of Jesus can actually become manifest in the midst of pain and difficulty? How does this process work? Have you experienced a time of hardship where you felt Jesus became real in your life in a way he had not been before?

Reflect on the nature of "faith" declarations we make. How often do such declarations turn out to be expressions of fear and not faith at all? How can we find real faith birthed within us even when times are tough? Have you experienced God meeting you that way?

Self-pity is the way of death and we need to be delivered from it. Why is it so destructive? Have you ever been stuck in self-pity and how did God deliver you from it?

CHAPTER 14

THE GATEWAY BETWEEN EARTH AND HEAVEN

Sarah Galloway

Most stories have an intriguing beginning, a happy ending and a moment of passing conflict in the middle. This middle matter is how we like to view suffering. A stepping stone to a brighter future. An intermediate, passing stage. So what happens when suffering strikes from the beginning? Or when suffering hangs around for a few more chapters in our lives than we would like? What if it is there right to the end? What if it causes the end? How can we place this perpetual character in God's bigger story? Where do love and suffering meet? Does it have a place?

My story starts with screaming. I screamed all night. I clawed at the sheets, naked and wild with fear. My parents were there trying to soothe me, silence me, any way they could. Even when I wasn't screaming, I didn't settle. I paced, I spoke to myself about suspicious thoughts and delusions that had gripped me. I cut off all my hair one night with a pair of scissors. I still remember the acrid smell of burning as I hacked at it. I still remember feeling nothing at all. Things only got worse. My aggression, insomnia and paranoia grew into a full blown psychotic episode. Irrational, disturbing, sometimes funny but mostly deeply upsetting behavior continued. Ten days, a broken window and a few bitten and bruised family members later, and I was admitted to a psychiatric ward under section. I was 22 years old.

Most life stories start with screaming. Screaming mothers, screaming babies, and the occasional fainting father. Life begins in a very painful and shocking way. This relates to Gen. 2:16, "I will surely multiply your pain in childbearing." Notice this says "multiply." It does not say God would create pain in childbirth. It already hurt. Whether this applies to actual childbirth or the process of raising children I'm not sure. Either way the physical result of the love between a man and a woman and their love in bringing up their children is painful. It's a struggle. So we see that the story of our lives and the story of love begins with suffering. As soon as you bring love into the equation, as soon as another person is involved, the door to rejection and pain is opened. Loss, jealousy, assault, extortion, abandonment all revolve around how we relate to each other.

This is not to suggest that God intends us to suffer. But he has allowed it for our time on earth. There is something in the process of developing a relationship that will always lead to some type of pain or compromise. The fact that the relationship between us and God has been broken only increases this pain.

I slept. Deep, unrefreshing sleep. Waking occasionally to play cards with my visitors. They were tired and wary too. Family and friends still adjusting to my cropped head and either very high or very low mood. I ate. My impulse control and self-regulation were shattered. I had visions of becoming a big, ballooned, bald whale. But I did not stop eating. I raged and I paced and I took lots of baths. I could not process what had happened, what was still happening.

One night I decided to escape and dressed all in black. Giggling manically to myself I ripped my tights to cover my hands. The plan was to get out through a window and run home. The plan proved to be fallible. For one thing, I was a twenty minute drive from home. For another, the windows were designed not to open more than two inches. I was trapped. For three weeks I was in hospital without leave. I was fluctuating so wildly that one minute I would be perfectly lucid, the next I would be ripping down curtains and bashing my head off windows and doors that would not release me. I was assigned a nurse who talked me through 'Wellness Stars' and 'Stress Buckets' and triggers — all of which was incredibly unhelpful. I hadn't been too stressed. It was a trigger-less gun raining bullets into my life with no apparent cause or reason.

Many things people say or do during times of suffering can actually increase our pain. They can burden us unintentionally in an attempt to understand or dismiss what is happening to us. Suffering can be unfathomable to those within it and on the outside. Often people view suffering in one of the following ways:

1. Suffering is a just affliction — "You have done something to deserve this." "You just need more faith." "Pray more."

2. Suffering is an assignment — "God is going to bring great things from your suffering." "God is just testing you." Sooner or later, suffering will turn into silver linings and lights at the end of the tunnel.

3. Suffering is accidental — "It could happen to anyone." "There's no rhyme or reason to it." "It is because it is."

None of these views tackle the root of suffering. They are things we believe or are told to try and make sense of what's happening. These can be meant well, but often sting like a thorn in our side.

I have been guilty of saying all these things at different times to different people. Now, I hold a different view on suffering:

4. Suffering is a sign of our separation from God. Paradoxically, it is also the bridge that heals this gap. Suffering has a unique place in life that both divides and brings us back to God. Suffering is a gateway between heaven and earth.

The reason we react so strongly against the concept of suffering is because we have an expectation and a vision of a world without it. In the Bible, this expectation is affirmed as God's kingdom on a renewed earth, where God will wipe every tear and end pain forever. The kingdom of God has started to come, but is not quite here yet at the same time. This can be a confusing concept, but relates right back to that statement in Genesis. In birthing children, we are faced with the greatest pain and the greatest joy in our lives. We have a mixture of the good and the bad right here on earth. God's goodness is present, but so is his absence. Because we are tangled in this good-badness or bad-goodness, suffering is even harder to process in the light of a loving God. But it is exactly because God has not fully separated himself, because he loves us, that suffering is magnified in our lives. The taste of hope brings a bitterness to suffering.

The doctors had no perfect answers. I was passed between diagnoses: acute psychosis, psychotic depression, bipolar disorder. None of them quite fit my array of symptoms: fatigue, emotional instability, loss of concentration and sequencing skills, bad short term and long term memory, loss of temperature control, a loss of cognition and reasoning skills, psychotic episodes and suicide attempts.

It was this last symptom that has nearly claimed my life on several occasions. My suffering has very nearly been and might still be the end for me. This can be hard to accept. Everyone likes the happy, hopeful ending where love and goodness triumph, and pain and evil are destroyed. But that is simply not the case in our life story. We are all under the curse of death. God is not just the God of the ones who overcome, but the God of those who are overwhelmed. Suffering is not always a test to pass or fail. We don't have to find meaning in it. Some things are simply destructive in this broken world, and grieve God's heart as well as our own.

Shortly after my first drug overdose I was approached to take part in a research trial. This involved taking and testing a blood sample for a certain type of protein. Less than ten years ago, a disease had been identified called NMDA-encephalitis. This can cause psychosis, and in extreme cases leads to coma and death. The name refers to certain parts of the brain that control how signals are sent. Sometimes proteins in the blood (called antibodies) can attack these control centres, and lead to swelling and brain damage. The test to detect these proteins in the blood takes about six weeks. In the research trial, they were simply trying out a quicker way of testing the blood. They weren't looking to diagnose me. They were very firm in outlining that I probably would not test positive, and if I did it was very unlikely that it was the cause of my psychotic episode. However, after a series of blood samples that came back positive, I was referred to neurology.

Diagnosis did not come quickly. From the other scans and spinal fluid sample they had taken it was not clear whether I had this condition or not. For a year, I remained under the bipolar diagnosis and received treatment from a psychiatrist. This flip-flopping of answers was a very painful experience. After a final blood test and over a year after my psychotic episode, it was decided that I did have NMDA-encephalitis. This came as a turning point in my treatment and potential recovery. But it was just the beginning of a long and difficult road. I was then nearly 24 years old.

An uncertain future is more painful than a certainly painful past. Though my experiences have haunted me, it is the fact that I simply do not know when my suffering will end that hurts the most. I cannot plan ahead. Suffering draws you into the now, the moment of pain. It questions God's fuller purposes for your life. These are my diary entries from 2015, a year after my diagnosis
8 November 2015

Some things are too horrible to bear. They're visceral. Shocking. They shake our very idea of what life should look like. What it should feel like. Afterwards, we are never the same.

I haven't been shaken like that. Of this I am thankful. But I have been slowly drained. Sometimes the uncertain future can be as sharp as a painful past or present catastrophe. Where there is nothing to catch the tears, no solid mark to pin the worry to, no name to scream, no wall to hit, nothing.

9 November 2015

I have struggled recently, in the light of all this uncertainty, with what it is to be called by God. I have heard so many stories of encounters and literal calls from God I've often felt slightly ignored. How can I — barely able to look after myself — be fulfilling the kingdom of God? Surely I should be on missions, or serving in the church or at least being awake enough to pray!

But then I have evenings and days where me and mum chat, cry and contemplate the world. Or where I ring a friend and laugh. Or text my sister. Or go see the fireworks with my closest friend. These little points of connection.

Just as the church is not a building but a people, so the kingdom as we now experience it is not a new world but a new way to live in community in our current place. A new way to love that transforms us. Like a moment of sheer pain that shakes us, sheer love will also leave you changed. It is a release of what God has put in us and around us, and not an invasion from the outside. It's something God is bringing within you right now, something already begun. So it's not something to wait for. It's not something you've missed. Just because God isn't speaking with a voice doesn't mean he hasn't spoken within your life. So feel free to stop always listening, and look around! What do you have in your hands or at your feet? Where has God planted you in society, in family, in strengths, in weaknesses? Where do they all point? Chances are that's your call.

We can still find calling despite our pain.

Jesus' call itself was to suffer. Ultimately, above all the amazing miracles and discipleship, Jesus was born to die. God suffered. God feared. God perished. This is the bridge to God. The gospel. Its simple power and unexplainable depth have only been heightened through my pain. I understand nothing of your suffering, and nothing of his, but I can say that one thing is true:
"In this is love, not that we have loved God but that he loved us and sent his Son to be the propitiation for our sins" (1 Jn. 4:10).

This is love. Suffering both comes from love and is its expression.

"Greater love has no one than this, that someone lay down his life for his friends" (Jn. 15.13).

Sometimes it is not obvious that we are suffering for love. Sometimes it is the absence of love that causes the pain. But Christ died for this suffering too. There is an invitation to a kingdom that can transform us not through our strength but through our weaknesses. Therefore we can rest. We can wait on God. We can seek his goodness in the land of the living.

Not all suffering results in good, but I believe good can always follow suffering. God is described as a healer and a comforter, both of which terms imply that some things hurt us and need to be fixed. We don't need to find good in every stubbed toe or bout of depression. We are attacked and drained. But God has unlimited resources for us. He wants to come alongside us. To comfort is not to make better. Notice in my diary entries it was people who gave me hope even though they were powerless to change my circumstances. I did not need a miracle. I did not need to rely on my strength. I just needed company in my illness.

I sat rather bored on a fancy, adjustable chair. I had a needle in both arms, one drawing blood out, the other putting it back in. The machine that was filtering it whirred softly next to me as I watched another episode of "Homes under the Hammer."

There is an inelegance and an anti-climax to being treated for serious illness. It is a long slog in an unknown direction. I have been on strong medications, had plasma exchange as described and also two types of chemotherapy. It has been a long journey. I am still fighting this disorder. I am now 26.

I still have bad days, I still feel disconnected to God and am unable to pray, I still live at home and I still can't work. But before God I can be all these things and still be valued, useful and loved in Christ. I don't have to strive or strain or suffer in my suffering. I can be frustrated, express my anger, give up, and feel the injustice within the safety of God's love for me. I am armed with the knowledge that he too has suffered and suffers with me. I don't have to be fake and "look well" before God. I don't have to try to be holy. I can rest. I can wait. Whether I live or die through this, whether it takes up every chapter in my life, I know God is writing good things amongst the bad. I know he is with me.

In the words of her parents Ian and Heather: "Sarah suffered for seven years with a chronic form of autoimmune encephalitis. She endured symptoms of pain, distortion of reality, memory loss and anxiety. Her symptoms fluctuated and in times of improvement she painted, wrote and enhanced the lives of all who knew her. The condition is not well understood and she was generous and brave in sharing her story. She died on the 10th July 2020 from unintentionally taking too much of her medication when she had a significant flare-up of her symptoms. She was twenty-nine years of age."

CHAPTER 15

SUFFERING AS THE BIRTHPLACE OF JOY

"Rejoice in the Lord always; again I will say, rejoice. Let your reasonableness be known to everyone. The Lord is at hand; do not be anxious about anything, but in everything by prayer and supplication with thanksgiving let your requests be made known to God. And the peace of God, which surpasses all understanding, will guard your hearts and your minds in Christ Jesus" (Phil. 4:4-7).

Sarah's story shows us how one person found the presence of God in the midst of awful and apparently meaningless suffering. Her closing words were these, "I know he is with me." The profound faith she carried behind those very simple words ushered her into the presence of the Lord, yet through her words her witness lives on. Sarah was a brilliant graduate of one of the world's finest universities — Oxford. Why God chose to allow her earthly voice, so powerfully expressed in the words she wrote, to be silenced, is unknown to me. What I do have, and what her parents and family have, is this assurance (paraphrasing Heb. 11:4), "Through her faith, though she died, she still speaks." As indeed she has just spoken to you.

Suffering does not create joy. Yet God can and does create joy in the midst of suffering. The joy is rooted and grounded in only one thing: the knowledge of his presence. Maybe, in light of our pleasure-saturated culture, we need to redefine joy not as a happy emotion, but rather a deep peace. And indeed in his words here, Paul starts with joy but ends in peace.

Paul, like Sarah, was facing challenges. They were quite different challenges, but equally pressing. He was in prison and his life was in danger to the point he was contemplating the possibility of his imminent death. He was in financial need. And worse, there were people professing to be Christians who were making life hard for the very man they should have been standing up for. Yet this painful experience of suffering birthed a command in Paul's heart, "Rejoice in the Lord always" (Phil. 4:4). What then is the connection between suffering and joy?

Most people spend a large part of their lives seeking happiness. Paul knew happiness is rarely found by those who make it their foremost goal. Why? Because, for one reason, happiness is dependent entirely on positive external circumstances. While there are always good things happening in most of our lives, they tend to get easily overwhelmed by the negatives. And there are always negatives. The day can start wonderfully, then be ruined by one negative word, email, text or phone call. After that, no matter what good things happen, they always live in the shadow of that negative.

The experience of suffering starts with that one nasty phone call, that one insensitive comment, that one inconsiderate action. But there is an alternative. Instead of pursuing a happiness that is focused on personal contentment or pleasure, we can seek the joy that comes from serving the Lord. If happiness depends on things around us working out, joy depends only on the presence of the Lord. God is not committed to our happiness, but he does promise to give us joy.

David was complacent in his apparent happiness, "As for me, I said in my prosperity, 'I shall never be moved'" (Ps. 30:6). Yet what happened? As he began to find his focus in his own happiness instead of the Lord, God threw a wrench into the works, "You hid your face; I was dismayed" (verse 7). God withdrew his favor. Things began to go wrong. But David decided on a wise response. He cast himself on God's mercy, "O Lord my God, I cried to you for help, and you have healed me" (verse 2). Instead of happiness, he found something better, "Weeping may tarry for the night, but joy comes with the morning" (verse 5). He found joy.

The goal of happiness is our contentment. The goal of joy is the glory of God. David's testimony was this, "You have turned for me my mourning into dancing; you have loosed my sackcloth and clothed me with gladness, that my glory may sing your praise and not be silent. O Lord my God, I will give thanks to you forever" (verses 11-12). His joy led to God's being glorified in his words and in his life.

Nehemiah hit upon the same truth. He faced constant discouragements in building the wall, not the least of which was treachery from within. There are few things more painful than betrayal. The arrows that come from behind cause the worst wounds. When the wall was finished, the reading of the Law brought a realization to the people of how far they were from God and his promises. An air of despair and grief fell upon the crowd. Yet the grief was a manifestation of a genuine desire to find God. Nehemiah therefore encouraged the people with these words, "Do not be grieved, for the joy of the Lord is your strength" (Neh. 8:10).

The secret Paul, David and Nehemiah all found was this. *Joy depends not on the changing circumstances of life, but on the One who does not change.* This is the rock on which we can build our lives.

Notice what Paul says, "Rejoice *in the Lord.*" He does not tell us to rejoice because we are suffering, as if suffering itself carried some virtue. Suffering ultimately is the product of our corporate sin and disobedience which through Adam brought death into the world. Suffering has no inherent value. But it does provide us with an opportunity to press into God and find true joy. Joy is found in God's presence, which is why, mysteriously, we can find joy in the midst of trials.

Our joy does not come from any external circumstances, but simply because we have found the Lord. This does not mean other things are unimportant. In fact, this opens the door to experiencing joy in all areas of our life. Our family, for instance, should be a source of great joy. Why? Because we see the Lord at work in our family, glorifying his name. Our job should be a source of joy. Why? Because we see the Lord at work in us and through us at work, glorifying his name. But if family, job, money, health or anything else becomes the source of contentment that we seek, we will not find it, because it has taken the place of God in our heart. And so it has become an idol.

Even something good can become idolatrous. That is why Jesus taught us that the kingdom of God must come before our own family. Houses, brothers, sisters, children and land are all thrown together into one great category of things that must be left behind in order to seek first God and his kingdom (Mk. 10:29). Jesus' words are almost unbearable, "If anyone does not hate his own father and mother and wife and children.... and even his own life, he cannot be my disciple" (Lk. 10:26). Yet in the same breath Jesus condemns the Pharisees for refusing to look after their parents. Not only that, he says in return, we will receive brothers, sisters, mothers, fathers, children and land (Mk 10:30). It is not that family is wrong, it is just that family, like everything else, is not the ultimate goal or focus of our lives as Christians. God alone is. If we seek joy outside of God, we will not find it. But if we seek him first, placing all else second, God will spread his joy through all areas of our lives.

How can God ask us to rejoice when things are hard? It seems like a kind of cruelty, yet it cannot be so, for God is love. But what if the command to rejoice pushes us into finding out why we can still be joyful no matter what our circumstances? What if in that there comes a deep freedom and a deep joy? What if suffering, which itself does not originate in God, nonetheless becomes the divine instrument to push us deeper into his presence? His presence redeems the suffering, even if it does not always in this life make sense of it. It is the treasure in the field, the pearl of great price, which is worth having, even at the cost of everything else (Mt. 13:44-46).

Paul began his exhortation to the Philippians with the command to rejoice. His next statement is this, "Let your reasonableness [forbearance] be known to everyone." This doesn't seem to have anything to do with rejoicing in suffering, yet it does. "Forbearance" ("reasonableness" is a poor translation) is the opposite of self-fulfillment. It is the attitude of care for others, putting others first. Those engaged in the pursuit of happiness often see life as one big effort to attain self-fulfillment. When suffering cuts across our quest, it leads to anger, bitterness and despair. The answer is forbearance, seeking the good of others before our own.

Personal fulfillment is the curse of our civilization. Martin Luther King Jr. preached the great words, "I have a dream." His dream was not about personal fulfillment, but about freedom and dignity for people. He paid for that dream with his life. But our dreams are much more mundane. They are about what we want, what will give us happiness, what will make our life easy, what will make us feel fulfilled. Tragically, this attitude infects the church. God becomes the instrument for our self-fulfillment. He is our servant to make us happy, prosperous and content. When he does not perform, we become disappointed and disillusioned. And don't blame your disillusionment on God. *A person can only become disillusioned if they have believed an illusion to begin with.*

God has a different plan for the moment when suffering strikes. In the face of suffering and challenge, Christians are to pursue forbearance, the care of others, just as Jesus taught us. We could call it embracing the cross. It seems counterintuitive. Our natural response is to cling to whatever happiness we can get, not worry about giving anything to others.

Yet it worked for Paul. God used the experience of suffering to direct him into a place of adjustment where he could find real joy. God used financial difficulty, God used unfaithful Christians, God used unfair circumstances — even being jailed for preaching the gospel. Many deep cries to God must have come out of Paul's heart in those dark days. And yet out of those cries he wrote these words about joy. He never stopped giving to others. Even these words written from a Roman jail have been a source of untold blessing for those who read them to this day. It would be a great mistake to think that Paul coasted through life on a charismatic high. How far that was from the truth! What then was Paul's secret? The pain he experienced drove him deeper into the heart and presence of God. And there he found something that, even if it did not always make sense of the suffering, at least gave him divine strength and comfort. He came out of it knowing God better, which is the greatest treasure of all.

How do we know that our forbearance is real? Our own feelings are not the best judge of how we handle suffering. Paul supplies the answer: our forbearance is real when it is "known to everyone." How do people look at you? Pressure, pain and suffering reveal the true person. At those times, do others see in you someone wrapped up in their own issues? Or do they see someone who, remarkably, is thinking of others even in the midst of their own struggles? Do they see someone who responds to pressure with anger and annoyance, or with gentleness and patience? Mature Christians are those who are kind, who are gentle, who are patient, who are concerned with the needs of those around them *even when experiencing personal suffering and disappointment.*

Next comes such a simple but powerful statement: "The Lord is near." These words bring us to the heart of the matter. They are the key not only to surviving suffering but to emerge out of it renewed and strengthened. At the darkest times in my life, of which there have been enough, I have cried out to the Lord the same cry, "Lord, let me know that you are with me." Not "Lord let me know I am a success," for in those times all I know for sure is I am a failure. Not "Lord, let me know that I am strong," for in those times all I know is I am weak. Not "Lord let me know that everything is going to be alright," because I know at those times that nothing is right. No, all I can cry is the one thing I know that in spite of all circumstances is true, "Lord, let me know you are still with me." And somehow in those darkest hours, he sends me reminders that he indeed is.

Many years ago, at the bottom of a pit of despair, I was reading my Bible and came to the verse, "Therefore my beloved brothers, be steadfast, immovable, always abounding in the work of the Lord, knowing that in the Lord your labor is not in vain" (1 Cor. 15:58). At the moment, the mail arrived. In it was a letter from a young lawyer I had prayed for at a church service many months before. The story recorded in the letter was that when I had prayed for her, she was instantly and totally delivered from a depression so debilitating she had been largely housebound and unable to work. Now her life had come completely back together again. She was back at work and engaged to be married. God's reminder broke my despair and transformed it into joy and thanksgiving. I have never forgotten that moment.

And it's because the Lord is with us that Paul next says this, "Do not be anxious about anything, but in everything by prayer and supplication with thanksgiving let your requests be made known to God." Anxiety means to *carry the burden of the future oneself.* No one who tries to carry the burden of their future will be at peace. They will be controlling, anxious, inward-looking, insensitive to the needs of others because they are preoccupied with their own needs. Time and again, God has taken me at times of great personal anxiety and put me into the life of someone else whose need is greater than mine. I suspect he's done that also to you. Why does he act in such a way? Because forcing me to put my own worries aside is the best way of freeing me from them. As I choose to show care to someone else, God meets me by showing care for me. And that care is what I need, for when I feel his care I know he is near. *Knowing that the Lord is near is the cure to anxiety. Knowing that he cares is the cure to fear.*

There may well be a lot to be anxious about — the command not to be anxious assumes, after all, that we are anxious. Yet there is an answer to our anxiety. The answer is this: *God himself promises to carry the burden of our future.* All we have to do is ask! Be anxious about nothing. Pray about everything. At the darkest hour, when it appears God has forgotten or abandoned us, he reminds us that he cares about us. *It is when it seems he is not there that we need to know that he is.* And if he is there, he is there to listen and to reply and to help us. God never hears without acting. And he will act in response to your cry.

And now comes the best part, "And the peace of God, which passes all understanding, will guard your hearts and your minds in Christ Jesus." The understanding (or mind) is the place of fear. It is the place where we ponder our situation, where we worry about what is going to happen to us, where we consider the obstacles we face. It is the place of depression and despair, of hopelessness and loss. We can't think our way out of this place, because in such times there are always more negative thoughts than positive. Neither can we feel our way out, for there are always more negative feelings than positive. *No, we need to be rescued out of it.* The peace of God does not rescue us by our analysis or emotions, it rescues us by his power. The peace of God is not the mindless serenity of the bubbling fountain; it is the very breath of Almighty God rushing upon our troubled soul to revive us and to deliver us. It breathes life into our flagging spirit and weary soul, and somehow overpowers and overcomes the negative thoughts and feelings, and lifts us out of the place of fear. It comes whether our requests have been fulfilled or not. It doesn't *give* an answer, it *is* the answer.

The way to be anxious about nothing is to be prayerful about everything. The theologian Karl Barth said that when we cast our care on God, the troubles that afflict us cease to be hidden and bottled up, but instead are laid open and spread out before God. When we're in trouble, our first impulse is to go do something about it. That usually gets us into more trouble. The best thing to do first is just to pray. Pray first, *then* do something. If you do something, then do it having first received the peace of God. Let me assure you, things will work out a lot better for you that way!

Why do I say that the peace of God is the power of God? Because of the way the verse unfolds: the peace of God will "guard" your hearts and minds. The verb "guard" is a military word. It speaks of a detachment of soldiers standing guard over a city to protect it from attack. The peace of God is safer than any fortress man can create. It guards our heart and our thoughts, our emotions and our mind, every place fear can come against us. God will place a military guard around our thoughts and feelings if we ask him, a guard no enemy force can break through.

And lastly but most importantly, the peace of God comes "in Christ Jesus." It's not available to everyone, and not even to someone just because they claim to be a Christian. "In Christ Jesus" refers to those who obey Christ and submit to his will.

If you want peace just to tide you over so you can live for yourself again, forget it. But if you want peace so you can live another day for God's glory, you can't miss it.

Sometimes we have to make a decision of faith that, in the face of hardship and despair, of hopelessness and anxiety, we will choose to rejoice. To rejoice is to place a higher value on our fellowship in Christ than on all the things the world has to offer, including the things we genuinely need. As we choose to rejoice, as we come to him with the desire to submit our lives to his service, as we determine to show love and patience to others, the same Holy Spirit who came with fire at Pentecost will come with power to build a fortress of hope around us.

Listen to the words of the prophet, "Though the fig tree should not blossom, nor fruit be on the vines, the produce of the olive fail and the fields yield no food, the flock be cut off from the fold and there be no herd in the stalls, yet will I rejoice in the Lord; I will take joy in the God of my salvation. God, the Lord, is my strength; he makes my feet like the deer's; he makes me tread on my high places" (Hab. 3:17-19).

REFLECTIONS FOR DISCUSSION:

Seeking happiness may be the most effective way of making ourselves miserable. After reading this chapter, would you agree and if so why? What are the challenges for Christians living in a pleasure-seeking culture? What answers should we as Christians offer?

"Anxiety means to carry the burden of the future oneself." What does this statement mean to you? How often do you experience it? How have you been able to free yourself from it?

Does it come as a surprise to you that the peace of God and the power of God are closely related? Have you experienced this in your life? How can we find God's peace in the midst of turmoil?

CHAPTER 16

IS MY SUFFERING CAUSED BY MY SIN?

One fateful day in Jerusalem Jesus and his disciples encountered a man born blind. The disciples, like most Jews of their day, assumed that sin and suffering were intimately connected, for they said: "Rabbi, who sinned, this man or his parents, that he was born blind?" (Jn. 9:2). In one sense, they weren't completely mistaken. Paul teaches in Rom. 5:12-21 that sin entered the human race through Adam, and has caused no end of calamity since. We opened the door to sin and suffering, and we are all responsible for that. And of course there are occasions in the Bible where sin directly affects someone's health. Miriam was smitten with leprosy because of rebellion (Num. 12:10). King Uzziah suffered the same fate because of pride (2 Chron. 26:19). Ananias and Sapphira were struck down because of their deception (Ac. 5:1-11). Herod died because he encouraged people to worship him instead of God (Ac. 12:23). But before we find out how Jesus handled this situation on the streets of Jerusalem, let's try to understand something about the relationship between sin and suffering.

We begin by making a bold statement: *the Bible nowhere teaches that a person's illness or suffering is always or even normally caused by their own personal sin.* Look at Job as the greatest example. Consider the illness Paul suffered in Galatia (Gal. 4:13) or his thorn in the flesh (2 Cor. 12:7). The fact is that when sin entered the human race, death came with it. The land was cursed, and so was our health. All the circumstances of life were affected negatively. But only in Adam's case was all of that attributable to one person's own sin. Every subsequent generation has borne the effects of that one person's sin. Paul teaches in Romans 5 that we are all responsible — we would all have done the same thing as Adam. However, the way that sin plays out in each of our lives is different. There is a direct cause and effect only in the *spiritual* realm. Let me explain. We sin, and, as a direct result of that sin for which God holds us personally responsible, we each suffer the penalty of eternal separation from God. But for that there is a solution, which God himself provided in the sacrifice of his own Son.

But in the material, emotional, relational or financial realm, sin is like nuclear fallout. It affects everyone, but each in a different way. All of us, even Christians, will eventually die, though for Christians death is only the doorway to eternal life. But someone who genuinely loves the Lord may be hit by personal tragedy — death of a child, cancer at a young age, financial disaster — whereas an unbeliever with no character whatever may appear to prosper in everything he does. The Psalmist grappled with this paradox. He complained to the Lord about the wicked man, "You fill their womb with treasure; they are satisfied with children, and they leave their abundance to their infants" (Ps. 17:14). As another Psalm says, "In arrogance the wicked hotly pursue the poor... His ways prosper at all times... He says in his heart, 'God has forgotten, he has hidden his face, he will never see it'" (Ps. 10:2, 5, 11).

This raises the question, "Are there consequences to sinful or to righteous actions?" And the answer is *in general* yes. If we manage our finances according to Biblical principles, walking in financial integrity and avoiding debt as much as possible, there is a much greater probability we will be in good financial shape than others who do not do those things. If we handle our health and treat our bodies as temples of the Holy Spirit, there is a much higher probability we will enjoy good health than those who do not. But can a financial calamity happen to a Christian for no fault of his own? The answer is undeniably yes. Can a health issue strike a godly person? Again the answer is yes. The hard fact is there is no necessary cause and effect between godliness or the lack of it, and personal misfortunes and tragedies. We would like there to be, for then godliness would provide insurance against all misfortune. But that is where we miss the point. We follow Christ not to further our own comfort or to erect a wall of self-protection against disaster. *We follow Christ so that God himself would be glorified in our lives.* Corrie ten Boom found strength in the Nazi concentration camps to show God's love to her tormentors. That strength became a testament to God's glory that before her life ended resounded throughout the world and won countless people to Christ. We must draw the conclusion that, although in the infinite and eternal purposes of God a Nazi concentration camp was the last thing he ever desired, nevertheless God used such a horrific situation to bring honor and glory to his name. Corrie was not being judged for some sin in her life. She was suffering on account of her faithfulness to Christ.

Are we then even to ask for God's protection? Yes we are! The Psalmist says, "He will command his angels concerning you to guard you in all your ways. On their hands they will bear you up, lest you strike your foot against a stone... Because he holds fast to me in love, I will deliver him; I will protect him, because he knows my name. When he calls to me, I will answer him; I will be with him in trouble; I will rescue him and honor him. With long life I will satisfy him and show him my salvation" (Ps. 91:11-16).

How do we reconcile all this? The answer is by interpreting Psalm 91 the way Jesus did. During his temptation of Jesus, Satan quoted the words of this Psalm. His interpretation suggested that Jesus could throw himself down from the temple (or do anything else he wanted) because God was bound to protect him. In other words, God's job was to make sure bad things don't happen to us. Jesus opposed him by quoting Deut. 6:16, "You shall not put the Lord your God to the test" (Mt. 4:7). In other words, you can't treat God like a celestial sugar daddy! But we can learn more by looking at how that verse in Deuteronomy concludes. It says: "....as you tested him at Massah." What happened at Massah? It was at Massah (Exod. 17:2-7) that the Israelites demanded God give them water, and said they would rather go back to Egypt than die in the desert. That is how they put God to the test, and what Jesus teaches us we must not do. When God becomes primarily the provider for our needs, no matter how legitimate those needs are (they could not live long in the desert without water), he is no longer for us truly the eternal, all-powerful God. We no longer worship him for who he is, but for what he does for us. And then the goodness of God becomes defined primarily by the measure of comfort and protection he provides for us.

Jesus understood that God's protection has to be seen differently. *God's protection is primarily a protection against spiritual harm, against giving in to the enemy in his attempts to make us compromise our faith and commitment to Christ.* God does give us a guarantee of protection: if we look to him and worship him for who he is and not for what he does for us, nothing that happens in our lives will ever cut us off from his love (Rom. 8:31-39). In the desert, Jesus was tempted by Satan to look at God the way the Israelites did, but he refused. He knew that the day would come when God's physical protection would be withdrawn, but as long as he kept his heart right, God would keep him spiritually safe and in right relationship with himself. Even when he was carrying the sins of the world on his shoulders, Jesus never lost the blessing and the love of his Father, even though he may momentarily have felt that way. And God's protection was proven when he was raised from the dead and seated at God's right hand to rule forevermore.

Do I believe that God protects us from innumerable harms? Yes, I do. Do I believe that to protect us from all suffering is the ultimate purpose of God in our lives? No, I do not. His ultimate purpose is his glorification. Paul put it this way, "It is my eager expectation and hope that I will not be at all ashamed, but that with full courage now as always Christ will be honored in my body, whether by life or by death. For to me to live is Christ and to die is gain" (Phil. 1:20-21). So should we cry out to God for protection for ourselves and our families? Yes, by all means. Should we believe that to follow God and base our lives upon his word will guard us from innumerable perils? Yes, we should. But do we have the right to demand he prove his love for us by shielding us from all adversity? No, we do not. And that is where we have to leave it, casting ourselves on the most solid fact we have, that God loved us so much he removed his physical protection from his own Son so that we might be saved from hell and delivered into his eternal kingdom. How then can we doubt his love and care for us?

Now let's return to the blind man and his encounter with Jesus on that Jerusalem street. Recall that the disciples all assumed that the man's blindness was caused by sin or that of his parents. Jesus says no. "It was not that this man sinned, or his parents, but that the works of God might be displayed in him." Jesus categorically denied a universal cause and effect relationship between sickness or misfortune and sin. And we would be wise to follow his example. If someone's sin has led to trouble in their life, allow the Holy Spirit to be the determiner of that. James tells us the prayer of faith will save the sick, "and *if* he has committed sins, he will be forgiven" (Jas. 5:15). If the person has not been convicted by the Holy Spirit, it is unlikely they will be persuaded by our accusatory comments. Those in trouble need our comfort, not our criticism. They also need our counsel. Never mind how they got into this mess, how can they get out of it? If they are sick, let's pray for healing. If it's a financial difficulty, let's pray for God to turn that around. If it's a relationship problem, let's pray for restoration. We cannot assume that there is in fact anything at all they have done wrong to bring their misfortune about. Godly people get cancer and die. Godly people get hit by cars and are crippled. Godly people get wrongly accused and have their reputations ruined. Godly folk are damaged in dysfunctional churches.

Jesus makes a perhaps astonishing remark here. He knew that the man's blindness was not ultimately caused by God. All sickness is ultimately the result of Adam's sin and comes from the enemy. Nevertheless, he said, it was destined by God to be used for his glory ("that the works of God might be displayed in him"). God wades into the debris of this fallen world to bring good out of even the most tragic situations. From a purely human perspective, it might seem cruel for God to leave this man in his blindness until the day Jesus met him, simply in order that by his healing he would bring God glory. Yet from another perspective, God was bringing an undeserved restoration. The man's blindness was in a general sense the product of human sin. The blind man himself, like the rest of us, was guilty of sin. That general curse of sin had affected him more dramatically than most. Yet the man's deepest need was not healing but forgiveness. God addressed that need by sending his Son into this world to die for him so that he could be restored to fellowship with God, and the curse of sin over his life could be broken. If that's all God did, it would have been enough. But God did more! The breaking of the curse through the coming of the kingdom meant that the power of God to heal was released in his body. In fact, one of the signs of the coming of the Messiah was that the blind would be healed. Isaiah speaks prophetically of Christ, "I will give you as a covenant for the people, a light for the nations, to open the eyes that are blind, to bring out the prisoners from the dungeon, from the prison those who sit in darkness" (Isa. 42:6-7). What happened that day was a fulfilment of Isaiah's prophecy and testified to the fact Jesus was the Messiah. And it was also God's answer to the man's prayers. He had not done anything more than the next person to deserve the suffering, but he had done nothing at all to deserve the healing. And even if he had spent part of his life blind, he would spend eternity seeing.

From our human perspective, all we can see in times of trouble is our own need. And then our expectation is that God will come alongside us and meet that need. But what if God sees our situation and our need differently from us? God did not define the greatest need of that man as the healing of his sight. His greatest need was salvation, a salvation we know he received through the confession recorded in verse 38, "Lord, I believe." Part of that salvation, for him, was the restoration of his physical sight. But by far the most significant thing God had ordained for that man's life was the privilege of being able, by his healing, to bring honor and glory to Christ. For that his life, which would otherwise have been forgotten almost as soon as he died, has instead been recorded as an inspiration for believers around the world for two thousand years. From his present place of perfect perspective in the presence of the Lord, I am sure that man is forever giving thanks for the fact he was born blind and thus became the occasion for such glory to come to his Savior.

How do you and I look at the adversities we face? Why not begin by asking God for his perspective on them? Why not ask God for faith to believe he can enter into our suffering and bring gold out of it? Why not ask him to help us see our trials in the greater light of his infinite mercy and goodness in saving us? Ask him to draw us closer to himself through them. Ask him to bring glory to himself through whatever way he chooses to deal with us. Ask him to open our eyes to see Christ beside us, in front of us, behind us, within us by his Spirit. Ask him for a revelation of his plan for you, so that no matter what you are going through, you'll know that his hand is on you just as it was on the blind man that day, to lift you up and use you, however he deals with your external circumstances, as an instrument for his eternal glory.

Thus will be born in you a faith that rises above fear — fear of hardship, distress, difficulty, suffering — and a faith that arises out of the knowledge that God loves you, that he will never leave you or forsake you, that he does have a wall of protection around you which has shielded you in a thousand ways you aren't even aware of, as well as some you can actually see. This faith will birth a determination to serve Christ and to follow him in every circumstance of life. It will guarantee your life will stand in eternity as a cause of honor and glory to his name.

In one way or another, Jesus encounters us every day by the power of his Spirit the same way he encountered that man in the streets of Jerusalem. Every day he turns our darkness into light. Every day he shows his mercy toward us. Every day he keeps us safe in the shelter of his wings. Every day he enters the tangled circumstances of our lives to bring good out of evil. How? Just ask the Lord to give you eyes to see.

And then, just as he did for the blind man two thousand years ago, he will bring light into your darkness today.

REFLECTIONS FOR DISCUSSION:

How have you looked at the relationship between sin and suffering? How often have you drawn a line between the two? After reading this chapter, what is the difference between a legitimate connection between suffering and sin and a very wrong one?

Has reading this chapter led you to a different or deeper understanding of the promises of God in Psalm 91? Has it helped to make sense of situations where you felt the Lord had failed to protect you?

All we can see in times of trouble is our own need. How do we break free of this limited and twisted perspective? How do you think the blind man felt about his blindness and the life he had lived following his encounter with Jesus? Have you ever felt in a similar helpless and hopeless position and found Jesus in it? Have you seen God to be glorified as a result of troubles you have been through?

CHAPTER 17

FINDING PEACE IN THE FIRE

Kim Jones

My story really begins in 1999. My husband Glenn had booked a three day holiday in Toronto to celebrate our fortieth birthdays. Toronto is a beautiful city. There was a marina and some shops close by. Glenn is a very keen sailor, and I am a very keen shopper, so this suited us perfectly! We opted to look around the marina and take some photographs with my new camera. We were crossing over a very pretty dutch-style lift bridge when I noticed I was struggling to take a photograph. Nothing appeared to be stable, but at that point I assumed it was due to the bridge swaying, not thinking it could be me.

We arrived back home, and life resumed. Over the next few years, there were occasional signs that something was not quite right. I was becoming more and more clumsy, dropping things repeatedly and falling over. The doctor concluded it was probably age or stress. I trusted God, and what was there to worry about with him in my life?

I had given my heart to the Lord thirteen years before all this. I had always believed in God, but I never knew him personally until I had a "road to Damascus" moment. At the moment our second son Jonathan was born, I heard God speak these words, "Come and find me." It was actually a terrifying experience. Thinking my distress was due to the birth, the nurses were all trying to reassure me that everything was fine.

Once home, I again started to think about what had happened in the hospital. It was a very strange and slightly unnerving experience. What did it mean? Instinctively, I knew it was God, but why was God asking me to come and find him? I pondered this over the next few days, unable to forget about it, even with a crying infant and crying husband. I had an incredibly strong urge to go to church.

When praying, we often do not see what is going on in peoples' heads and lives, and yet God is always working. Our next door neighbors at the time were Christians, and had been praying for the people around them. How often do we ask God for something, but never fully believe it will happen? When I asked them about if I could come with them to church one Sunday, they were completely taken aback and slightly rattled!

I started going along to church with my neighbor, and initially found it all very alien and difficult to understand. I did not know anything about the Bible at all. On one occasion, in an attempt to make me feel part of the service, the pastor asked if I would like to choose a hymn. Great, except I didn't know any hymns! The only songs I did know were carols, and my favorite is Silent Night, so that is what I asked for. A wonderful godly man, he never flinched and said, "Well, it's a lovely carol and I cannot see why we can only sing it at Christmas. It was the middle of June. That was the start of my journey.

God was still not finished with us. A year later, my husband Glenn gave his heart to the Lord. With God, surely nothing is impossible, something I have learned many times over.

We settled into our new Christian life, eager to learn as much as possible in as short a time as possible. I soon realized it doesn't work like that! There are times when you just have to wait, stand still and listen to God. I soon became involved in the Sunday school and helped to run the youth work. I even learned to play the guitar — sort of!

As I taught the children, I learned Scripture myself, memorizing verses that would later be of such an incredible comfort to Glenn and me. I knew I trusted God, but didn't expect to be tested quite as dramatically as I was.

And so — returning to my story — after almost two years of feeling unwell but never knowing why, the pain in my head became so intense I asked to see a neurologist. I was eventually referred, saw a neurologist and was told there was nothing wrong. At this point, I did start to question whether I was really just imagining the pain and various other symptoms. Another year passed. Things were not improving, and the pain was now so intense I could hardly move at times. I returned to the doctor. By this time, I was so frustrated I insisted on more investigation. He finally agreed to send me for an MRI. I felt assurance from God, but knew in my heart there was something wrong.

When I arrived for my appointment, the staff were quite dismissive — another busy day, another neurotic woman. I am not usually known for a calm demeanor, but on this day I felt incredibly relaxed. It has never ceased to amaze me how God is with you even when you don't ask him to be! After the MRI was taken, the technician came over to me and asked if it would be ok to take another scan, but this time a tracing fluid would be administered to obtain a clearer image. Again, I felt no apprehension or fear, just slightly irritated at the length of time it was all taking and having to have an injection. Although the technicians are not allowed to share any information with you regarding the scan, I knew by their suddenly attentive behavior that something was not quite as it should be. I was offered a drink and assistance back to my car as they informed me I would receive an appointment to see the neurologist very soon.

Again, life carried on. I put everything to the back of my mind, a very dark and deep place indeed! Although Glenn was slightly anxious and keen to hear the results, I knew that I could leave everything with God. When I go to bed at night, I hand all my concerns and worries over to him. After all, God is up all night anyway! Reading and mentally storing scripture is one of the huge advantages of being a Christian. The more we dwell on it, the more easily it comes to mind especially in times of discouragement or joy. In Mt. 6:34 Jesus says, "Therefore do not be anxious about tomorrow, for tomorrow will be anxious for itself. Sufficient for the day is its own trouble." In truth, we are not to worry about anything.

A week passed and I went along to see the neurologist. He told me I had a brain tumor. Perhaps you would expect me to feel shock, fear, be incredibly upset or even angry, and yet I wasn't. My initial thought was thank goodness they have finally found the cause of all these symptoms. By the time of this diagnosis, things had progressed to a very challenging time. Everyday tasks were becoming more and more difficult. I had a severe eye twitch, loud tinnitus, slight deafness, balance issues and very intense sharp pain in my head and lower legs. Despite all of these symptoms, I knew God was in control and I just needed to trust and rest in him. In times of great trial, or even small trial, God will always supply us with the amount of grace we need at that particular time. By walking daily with God and actually listening to him, our top-up will happen effortlessly, and we don't even have to pay for it! It is free, a gift. When Paul asked God to make things easier for him, God's reply was "My grace is sufficient for you, for my power is made perfect in weakness" (2 Cor. 12:9). What a contrast to what the world tells us!

I think the worst part of receiving bad news is having to pass it on, especially when you know it will upset those close to you. When you talk about a brain tumor, people often panic and ask why would God let this happen. Yet that was a question I never asked of God. We live in a broken world and bad stuff happens to us. As Christians, we are not exempt from the difficulties and challenges life throws at us. But how we deal with them should be a witness to those who do not know the grace of God. I found this to be very true as I witnessed the reactions of those who knew God and of those who did not. There was a huge chasm between the two.

Once my diagnosis was confirmed, I was quickly referred to a neurosurgeon to discuss the next step. Because of the late diagnosis, the only option for me was surgery, as the tumor was already starting to press on the brain stem. It was also an unusual shape, which meant it was growing deeper and causing more damage. A date for February was agreed. I did not want to have surgery any sooner, as at that time I was caring for my son Christopher, who himself had undergone major surgery on his leg. I wanted to make sure that he was alright before I went into the hospital myself. There are never any guarantees with surgery, and the risks with brain surgery can be quite severe. I also wanted to enjoy what could be the last Christmas with my family.

It was those around me who seemed the most upset by my decision to wait a further 4 months. But the type of tumor I had, an acoustic neuroma, was actually very slow growing. And the damage had already been done. The surgeon agreed that waiting a few more months would not make that much difference. My faith in God never wavered. If anything, it became stronger. I became much more focused on my walk with him. My thoughts tended to be more about how my family would cope on a day to day basis without me. Not that I felt I was indispensable, but after all I was the only one who knew how to cook and do the laundry! The kitchen belonged to me only, and no one else was allowed to use anything without prior consent (something true to this day!).

I had often listened to preachers recounting their deep experiences with God and how, when situations were scary and seemed impossible, their trust and faith in God always paid off. When listening, I always nodded and agreed, and often thought how wonderful they were to show so much faith. I would then go home and carry on with my life, and if I am truly honest, not give it much more thought.

But now things had certainly taken a sharp turn, and I realized it I who was in the scary situation.

With God, all things work together for good. I wasn't quite sure where the good was in this situation, but knew I had to trust in him. I knew that he wouldn't let me down.

Christmas came and went, Christopher made a wonderful recovery and God was very good throughout. Then it was February, and things did start to become a little tense, as we had to consider how things would be if I didn't come home from the hospital. The negatives of surgery had been laid out very clearly, and I did start to think about not being here any more. Praise God, in all this, I was never afraid. Concerned about those around me — yes. For me it was a win-win situation. To close my eyes holding Glenn's hand, and then wake up with my Lord and Savior, it was difficult to feel too upset.

The night before going into hospital for surgery, Glenn and I prayed for God's peace, that he would guide the surgeon's hand, that everything would go according to plan and I would be back home quickly. It was good to know that the whole church was also praying for me. I have never experienced anything outside the church like the spiritual intimacy of fellow Christians upholding you in prayer.

Being prepared for surgery can be slightly daunting. Like most people, the thought of large needles being pushed into your body is not a good one. That said, if you think about it logically, it's only a few seconds of pain, then euphoria quickly follows as the sedation kicks in. Something that has always stuck with me is how smiley and chatty everyone is as they wheel you down to theater and continue to carry out their various tasks. A captive audience means an ideal opportunity to talk about God, which I did. Apart from sharing my faith, it was also very comforting to be talking out loud about how I trusted God to see me through everything. Everyone smiled and nodded, and who knows, a seed may have been planted. As the anesthesia was administered, I drifted off peacefully, not knowing what the outcome would be but trusting that whatever happened, God would see me through it.

I have very little memory of the next few weeks. After surgery, I spent a few days in ICU drifting in and out of consciousness. Glenn was concerned about my level of apparent distress. The nurse told Glenn it was quite normal after brain surgery for the patient to be disoriented, but Glenn pressed for the doctor to come. He said the same. Finally, they gave me an injection which appeared to settle me down. Glenn demanded that one of the surgeons take a look at me, and then phoned the surgeon himself, who said he would come the next day. Glenn insisted that he come immediately, and he did. Shortly after, the surgeon called to ask Glenn permission to operate in order to remove pressure on the brain which had been caused by a bleed. The situation had quickly become critical. Even though I was ready to meet the Lord, Glenn did not want to lose me. I thank God now for his persistence! I pulled through, and was put back into ICU.

I believe God cares for us and even sends his angels to help us when we are at our lowest ebb. Even Jesus experienced that. There was one such angel in the ICU. The brain trauma led to continuous nausea. My angel came in the form of a wonderful nurse. I didn't see her face but I heard her voice, soothing with a lovely Irish lilt. I heard her say, "Would you like me to wash your hair?" I felt my head very gently lifted up as she then proceeded to carefully clean away the dried blood and debris from the operation. It felt as though Jesus himself was washing my hair. As the nurse quietly talked to me, I felt God reassuring me that everything would be fine. Such a simple act of kindness, and yet so meaningful. Think how Jesus carefully washed the feet of the disciples, a servant attitude we should all strive for.

Usually after brain surgery, patients become quite aggressive and inappropriate, but that didn't happen with me. I had such a deep experience of God as I lay in that hospital bed, I felt I could feel him next to me, his breath on my face, imparting his peace, keeping me calm. Again, this was an amazing witness to the nursing staff, as they kept remarking how peaceful I was. How loud God is in the silence! I had always enjoyed loud, vibrant worship while praising God. Now here I was praising him without a voice, in the stillness of an empty hospital room, and I had never experienced such an intense sensation of his presence. Those moments of intimacy with God have never left me, and have sustained me through what has been an incredibly challenging time.

After a few more days in ICU, I was returned to my room just off the main ward. Glenn would come to visit me three times a day. I was too ill to have anyone around for any length of time and it was very distressing for him to see me hooked up to several drips with tubes appearing from all parts of my body. As I was unable to communicate very well, or sit up, and needed to be fed, Glenn took on the role as primary care giver. Staff would bring in meals and leave them at the bottom of the bed, but I had no way of reaching the food or eating it unaided, so it would be taken away untouched. Glenn began to bring in more palatable food, things I could actually manage to swallow, and he fed me himself.

Due to the effect of the medication, day and night became one long expanse of time, interrupted by the constant monitoring of blood pressure and medications. I tried to close off my mind and concentrate on God. There I found order and not chaos, comfort and not anxiety. I felt God help me control my breathing and focus my mind. Although I was now profoundly deaf in my right ear, any external noises pierced my head. I often felt as though I was drowning and unable to control anything. As I lay semi-conscious, sections of Psalm 91 kept coming into my mind. I was unable to piece it all together properly, yet desperate to hear it. I was able to make Glenn understand by repeating a few words. He quickly opened his Bible and read the psalm to me, another intimate moment we shared together with God. He continued to read the psalm over and over until I settled down. I am so thankful to those mature Christians who encouraged me to memorize scripture! *Even when we cannot speak, he knows our heart, he hears our sighs, and when we just completely let go and sink into him, he truly does restore our soul.* Until you are close to your last breath, I don't think you can experience just how near God is. It felt like he was breathing for me. As much as I would prefer not to have gone through this trauma, I am grateful to God for allowing me to share in that amazing embrace, and that feeling has stayed with me ever since. I have a very different relationship with God now. I know without any shadow of a doubt he is with me. I have nothing to worry about, he is in control.

After about five days, they started removing some of the IVs. Everything seemed to take an age. I was unable to move around without becoming severely disoriented. Up until then I had not been allowed to look in a mirror, but now in the bathroom, I had the choice. As I searched the strange image staring back at me, I slowly tried to work out what was going on with my face. Nothing seemed to be where it should be. Was I melting? The whole right side had dropped, my hair was nowhere to be seen and I had what looked like a large metal zipper running up over the back of my head from the middle of my neck.

After a week had passed I was desperate to be home, to be in my own bed and rest my head on my own pillow without having to worry about pulling out any IVs or being woken up to make sure I was ok. Finally, permission was granted.

My stay at home lasted only one night! When Glenn helped me to sit up the following morning, my stomach emptied its contents. A quick phone call to the doctor was followed by an emergency dash back to hospital. All I could do was try and stay calm and rest in God. I was feeling too overwhelmed even to pray. I was quickly assessed and found to have a CSF (cerebral spinal fluid) leak. I cannot put into words the expression on Glenn's face. I was probably more upset for him than anything else. He looked so lost. I know he just wanted to make everything ok for me but it was out of his hands. We shared a glance and knew we were both asking God the same thing.

The next two weeks are still pretty vague, and I remember very little. The doctors tried a lumbar puncture to equalize the pressure in my head, but it didn't work. They had to open up my head again in order to seal the leaking mastoid air cells, then another lumbar puncture, but this time it worked. After a further two weeks, I was allowed home.

As I write this, it has been a little over thirteen years since the removal of the brain tumor. Life has been very difficult, and I still face constant challenges. The deafness has proven to be one of the hardest things, but I also have chronic neuropathic pain, severe tinnitus, chronic fatigue, nausea, loss of balance, fibromyalgia, impaired cognitive skills, trigeminal neuralgia, poor swallow and difficulty with eating and drinking. Because of this, I no longer like to be anywhere loud or crowded, my brain finds it extremely tiring to sort through and recognize faces and sometimes understand language. I now rely heavily on lip reading and I also use sign language.

It was not only me who was affected. All this has had a profound, life-changing impact on my family and friends, who have been incredibly supportive throughout. In everything, I am very thankful to God. He has constantly provided all that I need, in big ways and small ways. My husband has never once made me feel anything other than loved. Trusting God for strength for himself, he has also helped me to find new coping strategies in dealing with the pain and the constant basic life challenges I now face. He is always encouraging, but never pushes me when he sees things are just too much to handle. Our sons have been wonderful throughout and have quietly accepted all the changes we have had to make. My daughter-in-law, a speech and language therapist, is a great support — we always have something to talk about.

I still have many days when I need to be alone and in a quiet place, and this is when I have my closest moments with God. He never crowds me or shouts. Paul's word in Phil. 4: 4-13 have continued to be a great source of comfort to me. We can truly rejoice in him, find the peace that passes understanding, and know that through him we can do all things. With the Spirit of God dwelling in you, Scripture truly comes to life! Although Jesus is no longer here with us in body, he has sent the Holy Spirit to encourage and guide us.

My prayer for you is that you too would experience all that God has for you. You only have to ask.

Kim Jones lives with her husband Glenn in Great Lumley, County Durham, England

CHAPTER 18

THE POWER OF GIVING THANKS

Through a time of severe trial, Kim found a place of gratefulness to God which led her deep into his peace and his presence. This enabled her to be a witness to Christ in the midst of her suffering and in her community in the years since, as I can bear witness. The Bible tells us we need to be able to give thanks in all circumstances, and Kim's story powerfully illustrates how one woman enduring incredible suffering was able to do that. Her relationship with the Lord spilled over into witness even on her way to the operating room.

The story of just how important thanksgiving is began in the garden. There, we had absolutely everything we needed. Satan entered into the picture in order to bring division between God and us. But he had a problem. How do you stir up resentment against God in an environment where so much has been given by him? What he did was very clever. His strategy was to cause Adam and Eve to focus not on all the things God had given, but on the one thing he had not given, access to the fruit of the tree of the knowledge of good and evil. And he was successful. Ever since then men and women have set themselves up as the determinator of good and evil. This brought immediate division between us and God. It also led to lawlessness. How did this come about? Previously, God alone had determined the standard of good and evil. In his love and wisdom, God has the capacity to design a world where all of his creation benefits. There are no losers, only winners. But when we usurp the right of God to determine good and evil, right and wrong, something very different happens. In our fallen nature, we inevitably determine that good is what is good for us ahead of what is good for others. The result, which became evident as soon as the first people were ejected from the garden, was that Cain killed Abel because he determined it was to his advantage to do so. Now there is division not only between God and people, but between people and people.

And so we fell into a broken world without the capacity to tell the difference between good and evil. This has had massive implications on how we respond to suffering. If it is left to us to determine what is good, we will most certainly settle on a laundry list of personal benefits. Health is good, money is good, sex is good, a great job is good, and so on. What is bad is when any of these things are threatened. And in an imperfect world where everyone else is also seeking their own good, that threat is real indeed. The resulting suffering causes us, in our fallen nature, to curse God. The fall destroyed our ability to be thankful. Paul describes this very clearly, "For although they knew

God, they did not honor him as God or give thanks to him, but they became futile in their thinking, and their foolish hearts were darkened" (Rom. 1:21). And because nothing exists in a vacuum, thanksgiving is replaced by ingratitude and bitterness. And so people blame God for the problems which are in fact the result of their own sin. And this will happen right up until the Lord returns (Rev. 16:9, 21).

The promise of the Bible is that the curse over sinful men and women is lifted when they turn to Christ (Gal. 3:13). This means that we can regain the ability to be thankful even in the midst of suffering. And we can stop blaming God for what in truth we are responsible for. Paul wrote these words to the Christians at Thessalonika: "Rejoice always, pray without ceasing, give thanks in all circumstances; for this is the will of God in Christ Jesus for you" (1 Thess. 5:16-18). The people to whom this letter was written had not had an easy time of it. They had been seriously persecuted for their faith. They "received the word in much affliction, but with the joy of the Holy Spirit" (1 Thess. 1:6). Shortly after, Paul wrote a second letter to them, in which he said much the same thing: "We ourselves boast about you in the churches of God for your steadfastness and faith in all your persecutions and in the afflictions that you are enduring" (2 Thess. 1:4). In the midst of ongoing trial, they were described as people of joy, steadfastness and faith. One critical thing enabled this miracle to happen. They were a people who knew how to give thanks.

Thanksgiving is an appropriate response to suffering. This is not because we are called to be spiritual masochists, but because in the face of suffering our most powerful weapon is to thank God for all he has done for us. Thanksgiving brings everything else that is happening into perspective. It may show us that there are always people worse off than us. Or that God protected us from something worse. Or that our values were too focussed on what makes us *feel* good, rather than what actually *is* good for us. Thanksgiving is an act of faith in which we honor God. It results in God mercifully releasing the power of his Spirit into our situation to do more than anything our best efforts could ever accomplish.

There are actually three commands given in verses 16-18. The first is this, "Rejoice always!" Things were tough for the Thessalonian believers. Their joy was based not on their outward circumstances, but on the recognition that God had given them something greater. He had saved them from hell, given them new life, and filled them with his Spirit. They had supernatural strength, they had powerful truth and they had the precious gift of fellowship with each other. Joy is a gift of God, one of the fruits of the Holy Spirit, in fact (Gal. 5:22). It is impossible to rejoice in the face of adversity and suffering without the power of the Holy Spirit enabling us to do so. The act of rejoicing is not simply an action of our will. If it were, it would not get farther than the tip of our tongue. To rejoice, even in the face of suffering, is a decision to trust that God will enter into our circumstances and breathe the life of his Spirit into our act of obedience. That's why Nehemiah says the joy of the Lord is our strength (Neh. 8:10). Joy is a supernatural and powerful gift of the Holy Spirit. Through it, God releases his supernatural life and power into our weary and broken down lives to restore us and give us new life. But even more than that, he releases his power into the circumstances we face in order to change them. That doesn't mean everything amiss is suddenly resolved, though it is amazing what God can do when we turn to him with a grateful heart. As much as bitterness grieves the Holy Spirit, thanksgiving opens the door to his work.

The second command is "Pray without ceasing!" The command to rejoice and the command to pray are closely related. Prayer is rooted in a joyful heart. Prayer is the expression of our desire to have fellowship with God. You can't have fellowship with someone when your heart is full of bitterness and resentment. It may be a step of faith to begin to pray when things are hard, but as you step out, God will honor your obedience by sending his Spirit to strengthen and enable your prayers, just as Paul writes, "The Spirit intercedes for us with groanings too deep for words" (Rom. 8:26). Paul and the Thessalonian Christians had probably endured more suffering than most of us. Yet in the midst of their suffering, they began to rejoice and they began to pray.

Now we come to the final command, "In everything give thanks!" Notice how he says in everything, not for everything. Lots of bad things happen which God is not responsible for, and we don't need to give thanks for them. Yet in the midst of everything that is happening, the good, the bad and the ugly, we are to give thanks. The power of thanksgiving is this. As we turn our eyes away from our negative circumstances to the greater gift of Christ and all he has done for us, God releases the power of his Spirit within us. He opens our eyes to see his inestimable and incomparable ability to bring good out of the worst thing. If unbelief destroys faith, then thanksgiving releases it. Thanksgiving takes us out of the pit of our fear, self-pity and bitterness and lifts us into the place of hope and restoration. By acknowledging that God is good and thanking him for all he has done for us, it releases the power of God into our circumstances to begin to change them. *When we allow God to change our hearts, we find his power released to change our circumstances.* When we honor God and believe him to be who he truly is, and that what he has done for us is so much greater than anything this world can throw against us, it makes a difference. This is our stand against the same devil who persuaded us in the garden that what we had was not enough, who convinced us to establish ourselves as the judges of good and evil, who drove a wedge between us and God and between us and each other. *Thanksgiving undoes the damage the devil has done.* It applies the work of the cross to our lives. It releases joy and the ability to pray. It restores our relationship with God and our relationships with one another. Who wants to be around a bitter self-pitying person? But a person who lives in thanksgiving will always draw a crowd.

The passage finishes by telling us the greatest reason we should give thanks: because "this is the will of God for you in Christ Jesus." We give thanks out of obedience. We give thanks to honor God. There is always a massive benefit to obedience. To line up with the will of God releases the power of God into our lives. Our fallen nature tells us we should not have to give thanks when things are difficult, when God hasn't catered to our needs. But when things are hard is the very time we *most need* to give thanks. It's thanksgiving that releases the power of God into our lives to deliver us and to save us.

And even if there are trials, which there always will be, we will each have powerful testimonies to the experiences we have had where God has met us and encountered us in our hour of need. And if it is those trials that press us into God and enable us to find his presence, that is even more valuable than relief from the trials themselves. He is enough. His presence is enough. His salvation is enough. Today and every day. Thanks be to God!

REFLECTIONS FOR DISCUSSION:

This chapter traces ingratitude to its root in the garden. Do you agree, or do you see things differently? Why does one person see the cup half empty and the next person see the cup half full? How does becoming a Christian affect that? What's wrong when it doesn't?

According to the chapter, thanksgiving is an appropriate response to suffering. Is this a twisted perspective, or can you see truth in it? Why is thanksgiving a step of faith? Have you viewed thanksgiving as merely a positive character response, or have you seen it as requiring a supernatural empowerment as part of the breaking of the curse? Does God honor our thanksgiving even when on the inside we still feel miserable?

We aren't to give thanks for everything, but according to the Bible we can give thanks in everything. Have you ever stopped to make the distinction? Why do we give thanks anyway? Can you think of a time where simply giving thanks to God in the midst of a difficult situation brought a change in your life? If so, can you share what happened as a result?

CHAPTER 19

COUNT IT ALL JOY

Here is the verse none of us puts up on our refrigerator, "Count it all joy, my brothers, when you meet trials of various kinds" (Jas. 1:2). It's the kind of verse we hope applies to someone else other than us. But it's there for a reason! If we can learn what James is telling us, we'll be better off for it. Why? Because whether we like it or not, trials will come. James says *when they come*, not *if they come*. We might as well find the secret of how to encounter them successfully.

Trials put us to the test. By testing us, they bring out what is in us, for better or for worse. Pressure reveals the person. Trials come in different forms. Some are not really our fault, such as the persecution James' own readers were facing. But most trials take place when we are confronted with external challenges that are no fault of ours, yet reveal a weakness in our character. Such trials are the cause of most of our suffering.

This raises the question where trials come from. James is careful to say that God is the author of every good and perfect gift (verse 16). We should never say that we are being tempted by God, for God tempts no one (verse 13). We are tempted when we fall into the trap of our own wrong desires, which lead on to sin and eventually to death (verses 14-15).

When bad things happen, don't blame God. We live in a fallen world. The fact that the world is fallen is our responsibility and was never in God's plan. We invited the serpent into our lives, and have been suffering the consequences ever since. Sickness, pain and adversity of whatever sort are like nuclear fallout. They are no respecters of person. The rain falls on the just and the unjust alike, and so do the trials. Jesus addressed this issue in his own ministry. A tower in Siloam had fallen on people and killed eighteen of them. One school of Jewish theology held that bad things happened to bad people and revealed the judgment of God on them. But Jesus said no, they were no worse than anyone else (Lk. 13:4). All of us have sinned. Christians still live in the world that is fallen as a result of their disobedience, as well as that of others. God may protect us from suffering, but he may choose to allow us to endure it. The difference for Christians is not that they are immune to suffering. The difference is that God is able to help them in the midst of suffering, and even to bring good out of it.

Though God is not the source of our trials, he clearly uses them for his own purposes in our lives. James says that the testing of our faith produces steadfastness, and leads on to spiritual maturity, "Let steadfastness have its full effect, that you may be perfect and complete, lacking in nothing" (verse 4). God has an incredible capacity to bring good out of evil. He will take the worst things in life and bring some kind of good out of them. All he needs is our cooperation. God's ways are always constructive. He may destroy false supports we have erected in our lives in order to help us find a true support in him alone, and that process can be painful. But no matter what the outward circumstances of your life may be, God has a plan to redeem them.

We will encounter trials, James tells us in verse 2. That much is a certainty. The Greek word for "encounter" means to fall into the midst of something. The same word is used of the man on the road to Jericho who fell into the hands of robbers (Lk. 10:30). When trials come we often feel, like the man in the parable, that we have fallen into the midst of something out of our control, something we never saw coming, something destructive. When we do fall into these trials, James tells us, we are to count it all pure joy. And this attitude of joy is not to be limited to certain lesser trials, but applies to trials of all types (verse 2).

This joy, however, is not the same as our idea of pleasure. Why would we take pleasure in trials, or find them enjoyable? Joy in the Biblical sense is not simply a positive emotion. *It is an attitude we take in our spirit.* It is a determination that what is undoubtedly hard is destined, by the grace of a sovereign and loving God, to bring about something redemptive which would never otherwise have occurred. The emotion of joy is real, but it follows after (perhaps long after) that decision of the will. When we choose to submit ourselves to God and trust him, at some point in the process we will begin to see the glimmers of his plan unfolding. Two people facing the same negative circumstances could have completely opposite reactions. The believer sees the hand of God at work, whereas the unbeliever sees only trouble. Eventually, God will bring healing even to our emotions.

Our western culture programs us for pleasure. It is completely contrary to the mindset of our culture to see a trial as something positive. We fall into bitterness against people, circumstances or even God himself. We don't understand what is happening to us. That is why James says it is so important to ask God for wisdom when things are tough (verse 5). We fall into depression, anger and despair because we can't get beyond seeing things from our own limited perspective, a perspective that may be dominated by hurt, pain and disappointment.

Part of that greater perspective we need comes in verse 3. There, James tells us why we should rejoice in our trials. The testing of our faith which is brought about by suffering produces endurance or perseverance. If our faith is genuine, it will flourish and strengthen in trial. If not, it will quickly wither away. The word "endurance" goes far beyond the idea of the ability just to keep our head above water. *It refers to a dogged tenacity, a strength and courage which rises up within us by the Holy Spirit's power and causes us to stand.* It is a quality which allows us to stand on our feet and face the storm square in the face. It is what inspires soldiers on the field of battle. It is what caused Lord Nelson, as he saw the apparently overwhelming fleet of French ships approaching at the battle of Trafalgar, to raise his telescope to his blind eye and declare that he saw nothing he could not conquer. That faith is available to you and to me, whatever the personal Trafalgar we are facing. Many an ordinary person, when placed on the field of battle, becomes a hero. Corrie ten Boom, whom I mention often in this book, was a Dutch school teacher working with handicapped children. After being imprisoned and tortured by the Nazis, she was miraculously released. For years she travelled the world as an example of the love, mercy and forgiveness of Christ. She even led the Nazi guard who had killed her sister to faith in Christ. Suffering is the tool by which God makes heroes out of ordinary believers. And that alone is a reason for us to find joy in the midst of it.

But this endurance must finish its work (verse 4). It must not falter or give up. Its goal is maturity. When the winds of trial have blown over us and shaken loose from us everything not rooted and grounded in God, what is left is the solid gold of a tested and true character. Jesus was saying the very same thing in his parable of the two houses (Mt. 7:24-27). The one built on sand and the one built on rock experienced exactly the same shaking. When the trial was over, only one house remained standing. Its foundations were exposed as genuine and unshakeable. Adversity comes to everyone. If our foundations are strengthened through it, we are so much better equipped to deal with the next set of trials that come along. As time goes on, things that once would have shaken us badly begin to have lesser impact. Things that used to bother us a little we scarcely notice. Why? God has used our trials to remove the false foundations that we used to rely upon, and replaced them with new and much stronger supports. Not only that, we can use our experiences to turn around and help others going through the same kind of things. Our faith increases as we understand that God's ability to keep us in suffering is far greater than we ever imagined. How far this is from much simplistic faith teaching! The truth is that if all we ever got was positive answers to our prayers, our faith would atrophy. But it's when God allows us to pass through the deep waters that our faith in the end becomes stronger.

What do we do when suffering is staring us in the face? James gives us a very simple answer, "If any of you lacks wisdom, let him ask God" (verse 5). He uses the Greek present tense, which refers to an ongoing, continuous action. When we are in trouble, asking God must be a lifestyle. The statement assumes we do lack wisdom, and it's comforting at least to know we are all in the same boat. God does not condemn us for lacking wisdom — in fact, he is glad to give it to us, but we do need to ask. God understands what we are going through and wants to help us. He will give wisdom generously and without reproach (verse 5).

But there's one more condition. We need to ask "in faith, with no doubting" (verse 6). This seems contradictory, because if we had no doubts why would we need to ask in the first place? To understand what James is saying we need to define what he means by doubting. *He's not talking about psychological certainty, but about spiritual integrity.* Let me explain. He describes the person who doubts as double-minded and unstable (verse 8). To ask in faith means that our asking is without condition. That means if God fails to give the answer we want, we will continue to serve him regardless. The double-minded person will continue to serve God *only if he answers the way he or she wants him to.* In Gethsemane, Jesus showed us exactly what this means. There he prayed the model prayer of faith for those facing suffering, "My Father, if it be possible, let this cup pass from me; nevertheless, not as I will but as you will" (Mt. 26:39). In the words, "If it is possible, let this cup pass," Jesus was asking for wisdom and strength to face something that was a real challenge to him. Yet his commitment to God's will was unwavering no matter what the answer, "Not as I will, but as you will." To exclude every shred of doubt would disqualify us from ever asking God for anything. But to be unwavering means we choose to believe in the goodness of God no matter what the evidence we are facing in front of us and no matter what our minds or emotions are telling us. Our obedience comes from our spirit, not from our mind or emotions. *Our faithfulness to God is not dependent on how he answers us.* The prayer of faith is ultimately a prayer of trust that God is going to keep us, no matter what circumstances we are facing and no matter what the answer may be or how long it takes to come. *The man or woman of faith may doubt the circumstances, but not the goodness of God.*

My favorite prayer of faith in the Bible is probably the one I can most identify with. It's the prayer of the distraught father coming to Jesus for help with his demonized son. It's short and to the point, "I believe; help my unbelief" (Mk. 9:24). The father in this account had enormous doubts in his mind and emotions, yet he was not double-minded. How do we know that? Because he received a miracle! *James states categorically that the double-minded man will receive nothing from God, yet this man received a miracle from Jesus himself.* He did not come looking in both directions, as if to say, "I'll follow you, Jesus, if you heal my son, but I won't if you don't." He came to Jesus, casting himself on his mercy, knowing Jesus was his only hope, and trusting that somehow Jesus would meet his need. He wanted to believe – in fact, he did believe, yet he honestly acknowledged the inadequacy of his faith, but still came to Jesus for his answer. In spite of his weakness and the apparent impossibility of his situation, he had set his heart to believe, even if his thoughts and feelings were telling him the opposite.

The prayer of faith is a reckless prayer, prayed by reckless people. It is not for the faint-hearted. But it is a prayer that can be prayed by all of us who waver in our emotions, our feelings or our thoughts – if we are prepared to allow the deep peace birthed in our spirits by the Holy Spirit to overrule the confusion in our minds and feelings and jump off that cliff into the arms of Jesus. Why is it that trials are connected by James with the prayer of faith? Our human rationality tells us that we would be most likely to take bold steps of faith when things in our lives are otherwise going well and we feel strong. Yet such is not the case. The fact is it takes the arrival of adversity to force us out of our own sufficiency, the place where we feel confident in our own ability to deal with things, and out into that place where God alone can help us. Faith deals with the impossible, that which we cannot do. It deals with what happens when we come to the end of our strength and to the beginning of his, and the two cannot exist together. And that is one of the reasons we should thank God for suffering. It shouldn't take that to make us people of radical faith, but it usually does.

The power of God to advance his kingdom is released in people like the desperate father or the woman with the bleeding (Lk. 8:42-48). These were people who saw their time of suffering as an opportunity to cast themselves on God and believe him in an utterly hopeless situation. They came to Jesus in their desperation, and their prayer of faith released the power of the Holy Spirit to do the impossible. *The kingdom of God is not about attaining what is possible. Anyone can do that. It is about performing what is impossible.* And that only God can do. But he does it through us, and he does it through the prayer of faith. That prayer is somewhere in your heart. Reach inside and ask God to release it within you by his Spirit. Dream of doing the impossible. Ask God to set you free from the prison of the possible into the freedom of the impossible. That is the place where human ability ends and divine power begins. It often starts in our suffering. More importantly, it ends in the glory of God.

REFLECTIONS FOR DISCUSSION:

Has reading this chapter changed the way you look at endurance? Do you agree with the chapter's view? What is the connection between endurance and asking God for wisdom?

James says we have to ask without doubt, and he condemns double-minded people. Jesus answered the prayer of the desperate father who said, "I believe, help my unbelief!" How do we reconcile the two?

Have you experienced breakthrough in prayer when your intercession was reckless and desperate, and your emotions were all over the place? Can you relate this to the story of the desperate father?

CHAPTER 20

SO MANY BATTLES, SUCH GREAT FAITHFULNESS

Pat Westcott

My upbringing was pretty normal for a Canadian family. My dad was a bank manager, so we moved a lot. I had one brother. I started dating my husband Paul in tenth grade and never looked back — we've been married now for forty years. When I was 17, I got what was diagnosed as a severe intestinal flu and lost a great deal of weight, but I recovered and never thought twice about it.

I came to know the Lord through a charismatic prayer meeting in the basement of the Catholic church. Joan, Paul's mom, who was a Christian, took me to it. It sure was different, but it changed my life.

I was at college studying to be a dental hygienist when I moved in with the family of a girl who was friends with me at the time. They appeared on the outside to be the perfect family, but the truth was very different. The father was extremely abusive. It all came to a head one night the parents were out of town attending a hockey game. My friend, who was 17 years old, told me her father had hit her. To my horror, I was told that she was black and blue all over her backside. I told her she should stay somewhere else for the weekend, and I drove her there. Her younger brothers couldn't understand why she needed to leave as they thought their father's behavior was normal.

The only problem was that I had to go back to that house as that's where I lived. I had never cried out to God before that night, but on my way home I cried and prayed with all my heart, and I felt peace. As I went into the house, I saw my friend's brothers were waiting up to tell their parents what had happened. There was nothing to do but go to bed.

This man was very large and obviously violent. As I went to bed, the peace I had felt seemed to have left me so I prayed again. I was scared and crying and praying all at the same time! But when I opened my eyes, there was a light in the corner of the room and in the light I saw a large male figure. I should have been afraid, but there was no fear. The figure approached me, laid his hand on my shoulder and said, "Everything is going to be alright." I then fell asleep.

I got up and went to work the next day. I never saw her father again. He was never there when I was there, and a week later I moved out. It was not until six months later I told Joan about it. She told me it was an angelic visitation and that I should never let any one take this experience from me.

Paul and I got engaged a year later while he was attending Ontario Police College. We got married and moved to a town near Lake Huron called Wiarton for Paul's first posting. Our first child, Joel, was born in 1982.

Life was good. Joel had some physical challenges and both our families lived far off, so that was tough but otherwise things were great. We attended a really lively church and made lots of friends. We became involved with a discipleship group, but it quickly became apparent that underneath the outward excitement the church lacked the depth we were looking for as we sought to go deeper in God. We got involved in a new church that was starting. We had two baby girls in fairly quick succession. After the second girl was born, I suffered a period of rectal bleeding and was advised to change my diet. I quickly got pregnant again, and so when I was in labor with Josiah, our fourth child, Paul found himself recovering from a vasectomy!

In the spring of the next year, I came down with what I thought was the flu. I didn't really realize how sick I was, even when I couldn't get off the couch to make my kids a sandwich. Then Elaine, our pastor's wife, dropped by to pray for me. Elaine, who was trained as a nurse, took one look at me, and called Paul at work. Paul rushed home and took me to the emergency department of our local hospital. I was admitted and placed in isolation in case I had something infectious. But fairly quickly, the diagnosis came back. I had toxic megacolon, a serious complication of ulcerative colitis. My large intestine was ten times the size it should have been. I was hallucinating and thought my parents were in the hallway even though they were hours away. Looking back, the roots of it were obviously there back when I was a teenager and had the "intestinal flu."

David, my pastor, came to the hospital and he and Paul prayed for me. The fact was I was too ill to operate on, and without an operation I might die. Both David and Paul were in tears as they prayed. David went off to Toronto to a meeting, fearing what he might find on his return later in the day. Those were the days before mobile phones!

Paul and David had prayed that God would give me strength to get through the surgery, but when they prayed I felt that God had done something. Even though I was improving, the surgeon decided to postpone surgery in the hope I might strengthen further and be able to withstand it better. For the next two weeks, I was fed through tubes in my chest.

I prayed like I had never prayed before. I wanted to go home for my daughter's birthday, but the doctor would not allow it. I was placed on a large dose of prednisone, which is great when you need it, but comes with a price. I could hardly recognize myself in the mirror. My long narrow face disappeared overnight!

Eventually, I was discharged and went home. Dr. Moffatt, the surgeon, later told me I was one of only three people in the country known to have survived this situation without surgery. However, I was told I would be on the medication the rest of my life. I felt nauseated. I couldn't sleep because my heart was racing. I was exhausted. Eventually I went to the doctor and he told me anxiety attacks were another side-effect of the drug. At other times I was euphoric. I did my baking at 2 am. I redecorated my house by night. I drove my family crazy! I ran into another Christian woman on the same medication who probably saved my sanity by telling me she was going through all the same things.

We were so tired, with four young children and the physical limitations I was under. Paul, as I mentioned, had had a vasectomy as a result. But when Josiah, our youngest, was three years old, I felt God changed my heart. I then asked God to change Paul's heart. After much prayer, Paul went for a vasectomy reversal. After eighteen months, nothing had happened and we rested in the fact it wasn't God's plan for us to have more kids. That's when I got pregnant!

Jesse was born by caesarean section when his heart rate began to drop. When he was nine months old I discovered a white growth under his tongue. When he was operated on, the doctor could not remove all of the growth without removing his tongue. I prepared myself for the worst. The tissue had to be sent out of the country for analysis and the cause was determined to be a very rare form of infection due to a cut in his tongue. That was one of the times I prayed with no faith, yet God was faithful.

A few months later I was pregnant with Micah. I asked the obstetrician whether I could have him naturally. When I started labor, I went from three centimeters to nine in ten minutes. As I delivered him, I heard the doctor beginning to swear. I was hemorrhaging. Paul was holding the baby, not knowing if I was alive or not. My uterus tore from top to bottom as if a grenade had gone off inside of me. The medical term is abruption. There were eight doctors present in the operating room while they repaired me. But my life was saved. I had to undergo two further surgeries and took two months to recover. But I knew that this child we had fought for had a purpose, and needed a mom and a dad.

We had six children by now, and life was certainly busy. Paul was seconded to an emergency response team in the Ontario Provincial Police and was often out of town, and at the same time was serving as an elder in the church. I decided to supplement our budget by retraining as an educational assistant to work with special needs children at the local high school. I set my standard high, and put myself under a lot of stress.

One day I was throwing some clothes down the laundry chute and tried to say something to Paul. It came out very garbled and he asked what I had said. When I got to work, a good friend took one look at me and asked what was wrong. I went home immediately, called my doctor and he arranged for me to see an internist at the hospital. After a CT scan, he informed me I had suffered a hemorrhagic stroke. They offered to admit me as there was a danger of a second incident. But because there really wasn't anything they could do about it if it happened, I chose to return home.

Sleep eluded me that night. I prayed a lot. I had no further incident, but I was placed on dexamethasone, a drug seven times stronger than the prednisone I had been on previously. It's the drug normally given to people with brain tumors. Nothing could be done until I had an MRI and at that time there was a four month waiting list. I gained 60 pounds in a month! But God is faithful. I had to undergo a neuro-angiogram where there is a further risk of stroke. I thought at least I would be in the right place if I had one!

I was diagnosed as one of the twenty per cent of people who have a stroke for no medically apparent reasons. One moment from that time really stood out for me.

I was in the hospital elevator with Paul, and another lady said something to him which he couldn't understand as she had a neurological disorder of some kind. Then in the neurological waiting room there was a man holding up an X-ray up which had many nuts and bolts in his upper vertebrae. Another woman was walking with great difficulty. It was in that moment I felt God spoke very clearly through these people that it was all about perspective. Having a stroke was certainly serious, but my situation could have been a lot worse! I had regained eighty per cent of what I lost within 48 hours. The rest was slow but eventually came back. The neurologist informed me that if the stroke had been any larger I wouldn't be myself anymore because of where it had occurred in the center of my brain, where all the communication and fine motor skills happen. God is faithful! And I say that not just because I was getting better, but because that is who he is!

Along with the stroke I had all manner of seemingly unrelated symptoms. It began with a sore throat that wouldn't go away. Then I had an extremely painful shoulder that wouldn't get better, and after that I started having daily fevers and a rash. My joints would seize up and I could hardly walk. I was eventually referred to a senior rheumatologist in Toronto who diagnosed an auto-immune disease called Wegener's granulomatosis.

My need of God and his grace has only increased through all of my illnesses. I don't question that God heals. I have received his touch many times throughout my life. I have learned to live with pain alongside God's presence in my life. It's not easy, but his presence makes it a lot more doable! Countless times we have been ready to leave the house for church and I was in pain or massive discomfort. Time and again I would walk out the door before I would start to feel relief. It took a quite literal stepping out in faith but God would meet me!

Several years ago our fifth child Jesse came to me saying he had a small pea-sized lump in his armpit. I told him to change his deodorant and keep an eye on it. A week later he came back to me and said it was still there and thought it was bigger. It took two weeks before we could see our family doctor, but as soon as she felt the lump she was alarmed. Just before his twentieth birthday, Jesse was diagnosed with Hodgkin's Lymphoma.

We were devastated. We all sat in the living room and cried. I remember saying to him I want to tell you it's going to be okay but I can't because I don't know. It's a journey we are still on. After eighteen months of treatment with three kinds of chemotherapy, his cancer was drug resistant. He then underwent radiation followed by a stem cell transplant. That ended with a three week hospital stay where they gave Jesse 85 times the normal chemo dose all at once. The dose killed his immune system totally, and then they gave his own stem cells back to him.

Those three weeks I spent staying at the hospital lodge was one of the hardest things I have ever done. I watched him decline, then I watched him get better. It was a long hard journey and he was so brave. He recovered slowly and he was eventually able to go to college for a year, at the end of which he found a great job as a tradesman.

About that time, I notice a change in one of my breasts. I thought perhaps it was hormonal due to menopause. The doctor sent me for a mammogram. They saw a lump and did a biopsy, as they suspected cancer. After I got off the phone with my doctor, I had my literal two minutes of self-pity. I just said to the Lord, "Are you kidding?" Sure enough it was grade 3, stage IIIa breast cancer. I quickly had surgery, then started on chemo.

While this was going on, Jesse began to complain of back pain. He had a CT scan and his cancer was back. Two of us with cancer in the house at the same time! During this time our church family was amazingly supportive in prayer and so many practical ways. I finished chemo the end of January, then had a second surgery to remove all the rest of my lymph nodes in my right armpit. The surgery went well but left me with lymphedema (excess of lymph fluid). At Easter I began radiation, and at around the same time, Jesse qualified to be part of an experimental drug trial, as all conventional treatment had failed. Unbelievably, for technical reasons he was taken off the trial even though it had amazing results. More months went past before he was placed in a second trial. His improvement has been amazing. Eventually his oncologist decided to take him off all the medication he was supposed to have been on the rest of his life. And in the midst of it he has found a real faith in Christ. And a wife who also loves the Lord!

And that is really the bottom line. We are both doing fine, but we know our lives are in God's hands.

That has been the story of my life. It has been hard, incredibly hard at times, but I wouldn't want it any other way. His strength is made perfect in my weakness. His faithfulness is never-ending. I pray he would be glorified in days to come in my life and that of my family.

Pat Westcott lives with her husband Paul in Owen Sound, Ontario

CHAPTER 21

LEARNING TO REMEMBER

In the midst of numerous trials, any one of which would sideline most of us, Pat Westcott found peace and strength by constantly remembering the faithfulness of God. She faced the choice of focusing on her trials, or on how God had met her in them. And she did this in the midst of the constant mystery of how God allowed difficult and life-threatening things to happen to her, yet repeatedly and sometimes miraculously delivered her from them. It was my privilege to be her pastor during the long season of which she writes, and I bear witness to her faithfulness to the Lord through it all.

Remembering God's faithfulness worked for Pat, and it worked for me also. A number of years ago, in the middle of a massive challenge, I drove out to the waterfront to a place I often prayed. In that place, I cried out a prayer of utter desperation that God would deliver me and my family from a very threatening situation. And I asked him to do it by the end of that month. Well before the month ended, we had two miraculous interventions which saved our family and our church from untold grief. I often remember how God met me there. But the Bible teaches us there is more to remembering than just thinking about what happened in the past.

The question we have to face in crisis is not the reality of God's sovereignty, or his love or faithfulness toward us. The question is what our response will be to what we are going through. Will we respond with a trust which opens the way for God to do whatever he wants with us? Or will we respond in bitterness or anger, which will close the door on his work in our lives? Or will we be so filled with fear we will panic and make foolish decisions? Much of this depends on how well we have learned to see the hand of God in our lives. *And we learn through remembering!*

God told Moses to instruct the Israelites to recite the story of their deliverance from Egypt to each generation so they would never forget his mighty works and faithfulness. When they first left Egypt, Moses said this, "Remember this day in which you came out from Egypt, out of the house of slavery, for by a strong hand the Lord brought you out from this place" (Exod. 13:3). And when they were about to enter the Promised Land forty years later, he repeated his message, "You shall remember that you were a slave in the land of Egypt, and the Lord your God brought you out from there with a mighty hand and an outstretched arm" (Deut. 5:15). When they faced an apparently invincible enemy, they were to remember again what God had done for them, "If you say in your heart, 'These nations are greater than I; how can I dispossess them?', you shall not be afraid of them but you shall remember what the Lord your God did to Pharaoh and to all Egypt, the great trials that your eyes saw, the signs, the wonders, the mighty hand, and the outstretched arm, by which the Lord your God brought you out. So will the Lord your God do to all the peoples of whom you are afraid" (Deut. 7:17-19).

The significant thing about the Hebrew verb for "remember" (*zakar*) is that it is *a remembering which results in action*. For God to remember his covenant means he will act on his covenant promises to save his people, "I will not spurn them... but I will for their sake remember the covenant with their forefathers" (Lev. 26:44). For us, to remember the commandments means to obey the commandments, "So you shall remember and do all my commandments, and be holy to your God" (Num. 15:40). Remembering the great works of God and his acts of faithfulness gave the Israelites a framework or perspective, a way of seeing and understanding things especially in the midst of hardship or battle. The same God who delivered them in that battle would rescue them again. This was never to be forgotten by them, and was to provide a framework for their understanding of God. We also need to learn to recite the good things of God, how he has delivered us and helped us in the past, and to remember his goodness toward us. When we remember, we take the appropriate action associated with the remembering, which is to trust God for the present trial and continue to act in obedience toward him, in view of his faithfulness in times and trials past. When trouble approaches, we have a framework of God's faithfulness through which to look at it, instead of simply panicking and falling apart.

Twenty-five years ago, we had friends called Martin and Cindy who were experiencing severe financial testing. Reading their Bible, they found God's people being commanded to remember the past acts of God in their lives. And so they decided to put a stone into a jar on their dining room table every time God provided for them. The jar, which eventually filled up, reminded them of God's faithfulness. Not long ago, I had lunch with Martin and Cindy and found out they still have a jar on their table — and it is full.

Remembering the great works of God and his acts of faithfulness gave the Israelites a framework or perspective. It showed them how to understand their hardships and battles from a place of faith, not fear. The same God who had delivered them in the last battle would rescue them again.

Paul learned this lesson well. We know this from the opening paragraphs of his second letter to the Corinthians. Paul was bearing a heavy load of care for people he had poured his life into. They were no longer listening to him or following the way of the cross. Things were so tense he postponed a personal visit, fearing that it would lead to more division. Instead he wrote letters (not all of which we have), and sent Titus to try to resolve the situation. In the midst of this, he suffered a personal disaster in the province of Asia so great he described the effect of it as a sentence of death passed on him. Whether this was a life-threatening illness, persecution or grave crisis in other churches we do not know.

All this added up to what looked like total and cataclysmic personal and ministry failure. Yet he came through it, and apparently grew in the process. If you or I could handle this level of suffering, we could probably handle almost anything. The question is, how did he do it?

Part of the answer is that he knew what the Bible taught about remembering — "He has delivered us from such a deadly peril, and he will deliver us" (verse 10). He knew that the God who had delivered him in the past would deliver him again. Near the end of his life, he was still remembering God's faithfulness in the past as his security for the future, "So I was rescued from the lion's mouth. The Lord will rescue me from every evil deed and bring me safely into his heavenly kingdom. To him be the glory forever and ever" (2 Tim. 4:17-18).

We too need to learn with Paul how to recite the good things God has done for us. We need to learn to remember how often and in how many ways he has delivered us and helped us. And when we remember all that, we need to take the appropriate action associated with the remembering, which is to place our trust in God for the situations we now face, and commit our present and our future to him. He will not fail us.

REFLECTIONS FOR DISCUSSION:

Have you ever thought about the way the Israelites created those piles of stones the chapter talks about, or have you never noticed that part of Scripture? How good are you at remembering what God has done in the past? Have you ever tried to keep a record of it? If you have done so, has this been a help to you?

CHAPTER 22

SUFFERING AND FAILURE

Driving on an interstate highway near Grand Rapids, Michigan, I was feeling abandoned, hurt and deeply disappointed. I was feeling abandoned, hurt and deeply disappointed. Above all, I felt a failure. I rarely listen to music while driving, but on this occasion I put on a CD I happened to have in the car. Immediately I heard the words, "His love never fails, never gives up, never runs out on me." And God met me.

How God helps us in the midst of failure is the theme of the much of 2 Corinthians. As mentioned in the last chapter, Paul was facing what looked like a catastrophic failure. There we highlighted how he remembered God's past faithfulness and gained present strength. But the first chapter of the letter teaches us even more about his response, and it also teaches us something redemptive about failure. First let's look at the response.

The first thing and most important thing Paul did was to *focus on God*: "Blessed be the God and Father of our Lord Jesus Christ, the Father of mercies and God of all comfort" (verse 3). When failure comes, it is easy to sink in the emotion, tension and fears of the moment. We take our eyes off God, just like Peter took his eyes off Jesus when he stepped out of the boat and began to sink. But in the midst of severe trouble, Paul makes a declaration *not about his failure but about his God.* God is a Father, who will never leave us alone or abandon his purposes for us. He made us for a purpose, and no apparent human failure will stop that. He is a God of mercy and compassion. And he is a God of comfort. To comfort means literally to bring strength, and that is what he does, even in the darkest hours. Through his declaration of praise, Paul was asserting truth that would set him free from the prison of his apparent failure.

Second, he understood that *God was in the failure.* He "comforts us in all our affliction" (verse 4a). The word for affliction is *thlipsis*, translated elsewhere as "tribulation." This word refers to very severe difficulty. When crisis hits, our instinctive reaction is to feel that God has deserted us. The truth is God is with us in the bad times just as much as he is with us in the good times. *God will take us out of our troubles, but first he will meet us in the midst of them.* The proof of God's faithfulness is not how he meets us when things are easy, but how he gets us through when times are tough. God is not afraid of crisis, and he does not promise us that we will be shielded from it. Serving God, in fact, will get us into more trouble than we had before, and that includes failure. But God's plan is always to bring good out of it. For most of us, ninety per cent of our growth comes in times of trouble, as we are cast in dependency on God.

Third, he came to the realization that *both the failure and the comfort were not just for him.* The strength God gave him in the suffering overflowed into the lives of others. "If we are afflicted, it is for your comfort... and if we are comforted, it is for your comfort" (verse 6). We have the ability to help someone who feels a failure only because we have been through it ourselves. A Christian leader who never admits failure is not much help to anyone. Others are encouraged as they see us maintaining our faithfulness to the Lord in hardship. It is a powerful thing to be in the presence of someone who has passed through severe trials and emerged victorious.

Fourth, he saw that *out of failure comes hope.* "Our hope for you is unshaken, for we know that as you share in our sufferings, you will also share in our comfort" (verse 7). The word "unshaken" (the Greek word is *bebaia*) is a commercial term referring to a gilt-edged security. In God's hands, trouble does not impoverish us, it enriches us. The reason Paul had hope for his friends was that he had been through the process himself. That's where he got his unshakable, gilt-edged hope from. The only way to obtain this priceless security in our lives is through experiencing adversity, and adversity often comes in the form of failure. The hope is the assurance that whatever life throws at you will be turned into gold in the hands of a sovereign God, and that whatever setbacks we experience as a result of our faithfulness to Christ cannot be compared to the reward that is coming.

Fifth, he knew that *his seasons of failure were not random, meaningless or outside of God's plan.* Paul had received what he described as a "sentence of death" (verse 9). There is no doubt of the severity of the suffering. He says, "we were so utterly burdened beyond our strength that we despaired of life itself" (verse 8). The word "burdened" refers to an overladen ship in danger of sinking. "Despaired" means "in hopeless anguish." Paul was at the sinking point. When we are under this kind of pressure, we can escape into unreality through drugs or alcohol, and wind up addicted. We can tough things out in our own strength, and wind up burned out and embittered. Or we can turn to the Lord, and by his power and grace wind up strengthened. The hand of God is on us even in the midst of the worst life can throw at us. God's purpose is not just to enable us to survive. He has far more than a rescue plan. He has a strategic purpose, expressed in these words, "to make us rely not on ourselves but on God who raises the dead" (verse 9). *Achieving the goal of greater reliance on God is worth the price of any failure we experience to get there.*

Finally, as we saw in the last chapter, he knew how to *remember the ways of God*. He knew from experience that there is an end to every valley, and that God would deliver him. He puts it this way, "He has delivered us from such a deadly peril, and he will deliver us" (verse 10).

HERE ARE FOUR PURPOSES OF FAILURE.

First, failure teaches us we are really nothing. Life is not all about the achievement of our personal goals. The only thing that matters is God's opinion of us and God's plan for us. If that plan took Jesus to the depths of humiliation in the eyes of the world, maybe the same will be true for us. Never accept the world's standard of failure or of success. One of the worse problems is when those wrong standards enter into the church and into our thinking as Christians. Prosperity, ease of life, promotion, no challenges, no fears to face… to think that this is the entire purpose of God for anyone is a delusion. The main cause of disillusionment is because we have believed an illusion to begin with. We need to prepare ourselves for failure, while in the process redefining it.

Second, failure leads us out of our plan and into God's plan. I had a great plan to return to England, take a very promising ministry position I was offered, and get out of the dead end rut I had sunk into in Canada. God had a different plan. He kept me in Canada. Years of apparent failure were the result, but I hung on because I knew it was God's plan. Eventually I realized there were areas of pride and need for recognition that the failure was forcing me to confront. Dealing with that brought release, but there followed even more years of failure before God's plan started to come to fruition. Something in me had to die. I came to realize that God was using my apparent failures to reveal his sovereign plan. Now looking back I can see that God uniquely positioned me for a day he knew was coming. I had to be there waiting and preparing. God can take fifty, sixty or even seventy years to prepare a person for the last ten if he wants to. Even Jesus had to wait. My plan would have taken me out of human failure and into human success, but God's plan took me out of human failure into kingdom success.

Third, failure proves I am loved and valued by God. Even as Christians, we think of our failures as proofs that God has judged us, forsaken us or forgotten us. The opposite is the case. God loves me enough to use failure to deliver me from the delusion that success by the standards of this world is the goal I should live for. God loved me enough to save me from the kinds of superficial success that would rob me of achieving my eternal inheritance. C.T. Studd gave away his fortune and spent his life in poverty on the mission field in China, India and Africa, achieving little human recognition, and at the end of his life was rejected by the very mission he himself had started. He was a failure by the standards of the world. Yet the money he gave away financed significant Christian advances all over the world, and the seeds he planted in China laid the foundations for the greatest revival in all history. C.T Studd is a hero primarily because, by the world's standards, he was a failure.

Finally, failure proves we are children of God destined for glory: "The Spirit himself bears witness with our spirit that we are children of God, and if children, then heirs — heirs of God and fellow heirs with Christ, provided we suffer with him in order that we might be glorified in him" (Rom. 8:16-17). Suffering, including failure, is a privilege which proves we are God's children and is a necessary prerequisite for our being glorified. Why? Because we must follow down the same road as our Savior.

Failure reveals our wrong understanding and expectations of God. Failure is what enables us to grasp and walk in the way of the cross. Failure draws us deeper into God. Failure is the doorway to true success. If we walk this way, no matter what the human appearances are, our labor and our lives will never be in vain.

REFLECTIONS FOR DISCUSSION:

"The proof of God's faithfulness is not how he meets us when things are easy, but how he gets us through when times are tough." What do you think about this statement? Does it resonate with your experience or not?

Have you learned to see God in the midst of your failure? Has this changed your view of personal failure? Looking back at your life, or even looking at your present experience, can you see opportunities to re-evaluate failure as success? It's never too late, and may be life-changing!

"Failure proves I am loved by God." This seems an outrageous statement. What do you think of the way the chapter develops it?

CHAPTER 23

SUFFERING FOR DOING RIGHT:

The reality of spiritual warfare

Every Christian enters the battleground of spiritual warfare the moment he or she comes to Christ. If you are a Christian, you are a threat. You might as well have a target painted on your chest. Paul himself tells us we are called to wage warfare, "The weapons of our warfare are not of the flesh but have divine power to demolish strongholds" (2 Cor. 10:4). Spiritual warfare occurs whenever we choose to follow Jesus without compromise in the midst of a hostile and unbelieving world. There is a cost to war. No war can be waged without a price being paid in terms of human suffering, and spiritual warfare is no different. This kind of suffering comes not by chance or through our own wrong choices. It comes precisely because we have been faithful to Christ. Any presentation of the Christian life which denies this is a delusion and a lie.

Peter lived his life between two crosses — the cross of Jesus, and the cross tradition tells us he himself died on, as implied in Jesus' words (Jn. 21:18-19). It is not surprising he talks a lot about suffering unjustly as the price of spiritual warfare. "But if when you do good and suffer for it you endure, this is a gracious thing in the sight of God. For to this you have been called, because Christ also suffered for you" (1 Pet. 2:20-21). If we suffer for righteousness' sake, we will be blessed, not being afraid but honoring Christ as Lord (3:14-15). If we are insulted for the sake of Christ, we are blessed (4:14). If we suffer as a Christian, we are not to be ashamed, but rather to glorify God (5:16). He sums it up, "Therefore let those who suffer according to God's will entrust their souls to a faithful Creator while doing good" (4:19).

Anyone who has engaged in spiritual warfare knows the familiar routine: the day begins innocently enough, then it all starts to happen. One thing after another goes wrong, all apparently unrelated. A unexpected bill comes in, a child gets hurt, an unpleasant phone call takes place, a family argument erupts. Or things can be even more serious. A family member is injured, a marriage is threatened, a church begins to split, a job is lost. And so we begin to ask the question, "Is it worth it?"

And the hardest shots fired, those that cause the most pain, are those fired from behind. Paul could identify with that. His statement about warfare we started this chapter with is drawn from a letter full of pain. The church at Corinth, into which he had put so much effort, was under attack. His opponents were "false apostles" (11:13). They were arrogant men who commended themselves (10:18), and who boasted in their supposed visions and revelations (12:1). They were masters of deceit (2:17; 4:2; 11:3). They criticized Paul for his lack of authority (11:20-21), his poor speaking ability (11:6) and his lack of personal charisma (10:10). They represented a toxic mixture of religious legalism and spiritual experientialism. For a considerable season they made Paul's life a misery. The battle they fought against him, combined with struggles in the province of Asia, caused Paul a suffering so great he said he felt the "sentence of death" had been passed on him (1:9). His life and sanity were at stake. And the tragedy is this all happened in church!

Suffering for doing what we feel has been the right thing and being attacked for it has the potential of destroying our faith. When the hurt comes from those we trust, the pain can become unbearable. We are tempted to quit the battle. Yet this was a battle Paul fought and won. How did he do it? The short answer is this: he fought it by walking in the way of the cross. He did not bluster or threaten. In fact, he came by way of appeal, "I, Paul, myself entreat you, by the meekness and gentleness of Christ" (2 Cor. 10:1). *He did not allow either the wrong conduct of his opponents or his own anger and hurt at being wronged by them to affect the way he conducted the battle.* He acted not to exact revenge, but with their best interests at heart. He responded in love.

Christians do not operate by force and power — that is something Paul's opponents were doing. They operate according to the personality of Christ — his meekness and gentleness. "Meekness" is not weakness or fearfulness. It refers to refers to a strength that *could retaliate and overcome, but chooses not to.* It is exemplified in these words he spoke at the hour of greatest attack, "Do you not think that I cannot appeal to my Father and he will at once send me more than twelve legions of angels?" (Mt. 26:53).

The possibility of suffering for Christ raises a basic issue: how do we view the Christian life? What does it really mean to follow Christ? We would all admit that we live in a very pleasure-oriented, self-seeking society. This attitude can overflow into our understanding of Christianity. Do we teach people becoming Christians that following Jesus means to be rescued from all worldly troubles? Or that Christianity is a gateway to material prosperity? That their dreams can all now be happily fulfilled? Or that we now have a ironclad guarantee of protection against any harm? If so, we will have no framework for understanding the cost of spiritual warfare when that bill comes due.

So do we just need to resign ourselves to the fact that a lifestyle of love means a series of inevitable defeats and disappointments? Paul helps us out here. Let's go back to 2 Corinthians 10. Paul has been attacked as weak and cowardly. He refuses to fight fire with fire, but he does say this, "For though we walk in the flesh, we are not waging war according to the flesh" (verse 3). Paul's deliberate use of the verb "wage war" enables him to shift dramatically from the defensive to the offensive, but it is the *nature* of his offence that is significant.

The portrayal of the Christian life as a military operation is common in Paul's writings. It occurs in at least eleven other places in his letters. What is interesting here is how he handles the idea of a military operation against the principalities and powers of darkness (as in Ephesians 6). The battle, of course, presupposes human enemies of the type Paul was facing in Corinth. Yet Paul never forgot the real battle was against the devil. The first thing of importance to note is that the whole depiction here is drawn from the language of siege warfare, beginning with "the weapons of our warfare" in verse 4. The word "weapons" actually means "siege engines." This is significant, because siegecraft is an *entirely offensive operation*. Spiritual warfare at its heart is always offensive, never defensive. Why is it that we picture spiritual warfare as believers huddled behind shields while the enemy hurls spears at us? No, the truth is that *the enemy is in a besieged city which we are aggressively attacking!*

Many words in these verses have various meanings, but as Biblical scholar Murray J. Harris points out, can be translated as terms of siegecraft. These words or phrases are highlighted in italics, "For the *weapons* of our warfare are not of the flesh but have divine power to *destroy strongholds*. We *destroy arguments* and every *lofty opinion* raised against the knowledge of God, and *take every thought captive* to *obey* Christ, being *ready* to punish every *disobedience,* when your *obedience* is complete" (verse 4-6). If we translated these verse using these military meanings readily understandable to all Paul's readers, the translation would read as follows, "For the siege engines of our military campaign are not the siege engines of the world, but are powerful for the demolition of fortresses. We demolish bastions of argumentation and every raised rampart that sets itself up against the knowledge of God; we carry off into captivity every battle plan in subjection to Christ; and we stand as soldiers at the ready to punish any insubordination once your subjection is complete." Paul's readers would have heard both meanings as they read his words, and they would have got his point!

The enemy is pictured as shut up within a fortress which is being besieged by the forces of God's kingdom. Our mentality needs to shift from being the helpless victims of relentless demonic attack to being the aggressive adversaries of the enemy, pursuing him into his strongholds in a search and destroy operation.

If we see the devil as our true enemy, it releases us to respond to our human enemies with love. Fighting fire with fire, which Christians too often do, causes us to sink to the level our opponents are operating on. The thinking and actions of the kingdom of darkness must be opposed with the thinking and actions of the kingdom of God. *It is the very act of our love toward others in the face of the suffering they have caused us which releases the power of God on our behalf, just as surely as the cross released the power behind the resurrection!* This is what Prof. G.K. Beale frequently calls the "ironic victory" of believers. It hinges on the understanding that a man hanging on a Roman cross was not a helpless victim, but at that very moment was ruling over the universe and changing the course of history. No wonder the New Testament describes the message of the gospel as a "mystery" (Rom. 16:25).

When we face suffering because of our faith, we should come with some expectations in place:

A battle presumes an opposing power.
This opposition will do some damage to us.
The moment this damage occurs is the critical point where we must trust God and hold fast our position.
No matter what the ups and downs of the battle, God guarantees ultimate victory.
The fact we are attacked is a good sign in that it shows we are a threat to the enemy, and must be doing something right.
The love of Jesus is our most powerful weapon, in life or in death.

If we present the Christian life in terms of benefits and protection, the result — paradoxically — will be fear. Why? Because when trouble comes, we will have no frame of reference to understand or cope with it. "Why is this happening when we thought God would protect us?" That is why ultimately a movement that preaches faith and prosperity will produce disillusionment and disappointment.

But if we present the Christian life in terms of a battle which we fight offensively in spite of or even because of the suffering we endure, the result will be peace. Why? Because we have an eternal perspective. We know that the earthly cost is far outweighed by the eternal benefit. And we know that even in this world, our sacrifice has released the power of God to further a kingdom that advances through the way of the cross.

In the midst of failure, Paul had found the way to victory.

REFLECTIONS FOR DISCUSSION:

Can you identify with the chapter's description of the way spiritual warfare hits us in our daily lives? Can you share an example? How can identifying the difference between random events and hardships and deliberate spiritual warfare help us to cope with and respond to what is happening?

"The fact we are attacked is a good sign in that it shows we are a threat to the enemy and must be doing something right." Can you identify with this statement? Have you ever used this line of thinking to encourage yourself?

An old chorus says, "They'll know we are Christians by our love." How often do we fall short of this standard? Where in your experience have believers taken a wrong turn by "fighting fire with fire?" Can we hold our convictions without compromise, while at the same time loving those who oppose us? What practical things can we do to work this out in our personal lives, churches and communities?

DAVID CAMPBELL

THE LAST WORD

The last word comes, appropriately, from the last book.

The book of Revelation has been greatly misunderstood. In the process of trying mistakenly to make the book fit into the latest news reports from the middle east, the real messages of the book have been lost. And one of these deals with suffering.

Revelation was written to a suffering church. In the last years of the first century, the Roman Emperors began to demand that citizens worship them as gods. Various civic celebrations and rituals were organized to that end, and this was particularly the case in the province of Asia where the seven churches addressed in chapters 2 and 3 were located. Those who refused to participate suffered economically and socially, and some lost their lives.

John reminded his readers that the kingly reign of Christ is exercised in what we might call an ironic manner. Put simply, the rule of Christ over human history was never more fully exercised than when he was hanging helplessly on a Roman cross. And as his followers, we share in this rule. At the beginning of the letter, John described himself as "your brother and partner in the tribulation and the kingdom and the patient endurance that are in Jesus" (Rev. 1:9).

John paints an apparently mysterious picture of the temple in chapter 11, where the inner court is measured, but the outer court is handed over to be trampled for a period of time. The measuring refers to protection. It is similar in meaning to the sealing of chapter 7, and goes back to a similar picture in Ezekiel, which itself reflects the mark of the lamb's blood at the Passover, which in turn is rooted in the mark of protection placed on Cain. The inner court represents the spiritual life of believers in Christ, whereas the outer court describes our interaction with the pagan world in which we live. The meaning is that Christians will be protected in their walk with the Lord, even though they will be subject to temptation, suffering and even death as they walk the streets of this fallen world.

The narrative also tells us, however, that the present evil actions of unbelievers are laying the basis for their eventual defeat and judgment. The dragon was poised to destroy the offspring of the woman (chapter 12), but the child (Jesus) was caught up to heaven, and as a result the devil and his agents are cast down to earth, where they exercise a limited power subject to the sovereign counsel of God. The very place at which it appeared Satan had gained his ultimate victory became the place of his total and irrevocable defeat.

Under pressure, some of the Christians to whom John was writing began to compromise. This is what is represented by the references to the followers of Balaam, Jezebel and the Nicolaitans in the messages to the seven churches. All three groups, like the Biblical Balaam and Jezebel, pushed believers into compromise with the ungodly and idolatrous demands of the surrounding culture. The immediate benefit of avoiding persecution came at a great cost to their faith.

The opening of the fifth seal reveals the souls of those slain for their faith crying out to God for justice (6:9-11). The ultimate answer to their cry is given in chapter 19, where the great multitude in heaven gives thanks to God for the exercise of his judgment on the wicked and the avenging of the blood of his servants. The climax of the book is the portrayal of the new Jerusalem in chapters 21-22. The righteous who have suffered gain an indescribably wonderful eternal reward, while their persecutors are cast into an equally eternal lake of fire.

One of the main purposes of Revelation is thus to exhort believers to remain faithful to Christ in spite of present sufferings caused by their refusal to engage in compromise with the world system. Their faithfulness will eventually be rewarded in the new Jerusalem.

After the portrayal of the heavenly kingdom in 21:1-22:5, the final words of the book revert to the command to remain faithful. The heavenly visions serve as motivators for Christians now suffering in adversity to hold to the glorious promises of God and not to fall away. And so in the same way, like the saints to whom John wrote, Christians today should read Revelation and allow its portrayal of the divine majesty to motivate us to continued faithfulness regardless of the cost.

And in a wider sense, this tells us that whatever we suffer in this life, whether it be on account of our faith or whether it be simply as a result of the fallenness of the world in which we live, the reward that awaits us is greater. Holding this vision daily before us strengthens us to give glory to God and continue to serve him faithfully by his grace, irrespective of the challenges we face.

Walking in the light of eternity is more difficult than ever in a materialistic culture where comfort and wealth are valued above everything else, and where the human ideal becomes the extension of this present life as long as possible.

But for us, the words of Paul are still as valid as ever, "For to me, to live is Christ, and to die is gain" (Phil. 1:21). To the extent we can grasp this truth by revelation of the Holy Spirit within us, we will be those the last pages of the Bible describe as the overcomers who receive the promises of God.

And that, in the end, is the final answer for all who suffer.

ABOUT THE AUTHOR

David Campbell was raised near Toronto and holds three degrees in theology from the University of Toronto and the University of Durham, England. He and his wife, Elaine, have planted churches in the UK and Canada. David has also taught internationally in churches, Bible colleges and leadership training centers in the USA, the UK, Canada and India. He is the co-author (with GK Beale) of A Shorter Commentary on Revelation, and the author of Mystery Explained: A Simple Guide to Revelation. After thirty-eight years of marriage, David and Elaine have eight children and seven grandchildren.

Landmarks
A Comprehensive Look at the Foundations of Faith

By David Campbell

FIND THE WONDER IN HIS INCREDIBLE PLAN

Landmarks by David Campbell charts our course from the Word of God to our everyday lives. Each marker on this trail of bread crumbs reminds us of an essential truth that has shaped our knowledge of God and his plan. This is not a history book or an opinion piece; it's a compendium of foundational belief that celebrates monumental breakthroughs in christian understanding. Reading through Landmarks will leave you enlightened, grateful and strengthened in your faith.

Other titles by David Campbell

No Diving
*10 ways to avoid
the shallow end of your faith
and go deeper into the Bible*

By David Campbell

Mystery Explained
A Simple Guide to Revelation

By David Campbell

The Book of Revelation
A Shorter Exegetical Commentary

By G.K. Beale
With David Campbell

www.ingramcontent.com/pod-product-compliance
Lightning Source LLC
Chambersburg PA
CBHW072151100526
44589CB00015B/2182